Neil J. Anderson

ACTIVE

Skills for Reading: Book 3

HEINLE & HEINLE

THOMSON LEARNING

Australia · Canada · Mexico · Singapore · Spain · United Kingdom · United States

HEINLE & HEINLE

THOMSON LEARNING

Publisher, Global ELT: Christopher Wenger
Editorial Manager: Sean Bermingham
Development Editors: Maria O'Conor, Ross Wallace
Contributing Editor: Nancy Douglas
Production Editor: Tan Jin Hock
ELT Directors: John Lowe (Asia),
   Francisco Lozano (Latin America)

Executive Marketing Manager: Amy Mabley
Marketing Managers: Utzuinic Garcés, Ian Martin
Interior/Cover Design: Christopher Hanzie, TYA Inc.
Illustrations: Cue Art & Design Associates
Composition: Stella Tan, TYA Inc.
Printer: Seng Lee Press

Unless otherwise stated, all photos are from PhotoDisc, Inc. Digital Imagery © copyright 2002 PhotoDisc, Inc. Photos from other sources: page 97: © Reuters/Photo by HO; page 103: © Reuters/Photo by HO; page 115: © Reuters/Photo by Shamil Zhumatov; page 139: © Bettman/CORBIS; page 169: © Bettman/CORBIS; page 175: © Reuters/Photo by HO; page 181, left: © Reuters/Photo by Peter Morgan; page 181, right: © Hulton-Deutsch Collection/CORBIS; page 187: © EyeWire

da Vinci™ Surgical System (page 99) is a registered trademark of Intuitive Surgical, Inc. Guinness World Records™ (page 146) is a registered trademark of Guinness World Records Limited. Academy Award® (page 177) is a trademark and service mark of the Academy of Motion Picture Arts and Sciences.

Sources of information: space tourism statistics (page 116), http://www.gwu.edu/~spctour/market.html; childbirth statistics (page 123), http://www.babyworld.co.uk/features/one_child_families.htm

Every effort has been made to trace all sources of illustrations/photos/information in this book, but if any have been inadvertently overlooked, the publisher will be pleased to make the necessary arrangements at the first opportunity.

ISBN 0-8384-2611-5

Printed in Singapore
1 2 3 4 5 6 05 04 03 02

Dedication & Acknowledgments

I dedicate this book to my family, especially my daughter Amelia. Amy played a key role in the development of ideas for the reading passages in the book. Without her help I could not have written this book.

In May 2000, I was sitting at a swimming pool in Melaka, Malaysia, with my colleague and friend David Nunan, and John Lowe from Thomson Learning. We started talking about my interest in reading, and in the lack of a good EFL reading series. That's when the idea for ACTIVE Skills for Reading began. Chris Wenger from Thomson Learning initiated conversations with me, and played a key role in the early development of this project. Meetings followed in Seoul, Korea, in 2001 with Maria O'Conor, the development editor for the project, who successfully propelled the concept into full development. This has been a very engaging and exciting project to be involved in. It would not have proceeded as it has done without the work of Nancy Douglas. Thank you, Nancy, for helping to shape my ideas into solid reading activities. Mark Wolfersberger and Susannah MacKay also played a key role in the development of this book. They assisted in identifying content material, and in putting together the Teacher's Manual. These two young professionals will soon be writing materials of their own.

My family continues to provide support. Kathy, Cameron, Lisa, Todd, Kara, Amy, Ryan, and Douglas all watched the early page drafts come off the printer, and were joyous when they took real shape. THANK YOU for your support!

My hope is that EFL teachers around the world can use this series as a way to engage their learners in the active and strategic skills of reading. I hope that learners become better readers, and are able to use their improved skills to accomplish their life goals, using English as their tool.

I appreciate enormously the input we received from teachers in Korea, Taiwan, and Japan. We also received valuable comments from teachers in the U.S., Canada, Mexico, and Turkey. Many thanks to those teachers listed below.

Neil J. Anderson

Penny Allan	Languages Institute, Mount Royal College, Alberta, Canada
Jeremy Bishop	Ehwa Women's University, Seoul, Korea
William E. Brazda	Long Beach City College, California, U.S.A.
Michelle Buuck	Centennial College, Ontario, Canada
Chih-min Chou	National Chengchi University, Taipei, Taiwan
Karen Cronin	Shinjuku, Tokyo, Japan
Marta O. Dmytrenko-Ahrabian	Wayne State University, English Language Institute, Detroit, Michigan, U.S.A.
James Goddard	Kwansei University, Osaka, Japan
Ann-Marie Hadzima	National Taiwan University, Taipei, Taiwan
Diane Hawley Nagatomo	Ochanomizu University, Tokyo, Japan
Carolyn Ho	North Harris College, Houston, Texas, U.S.A.
Feng-Sheng Hung	National Kaohsiung First University of Science and Technology, Kaohsiung, Taiwan
Yuko Iwata	Tokai University, Foreign Language Center, Kanagawa, Japan
Johanna E. Katchen	National Tsing Hua University, Department of Foreign Languages, Hsinchu, Taiwan
Peter Kipp	Ehwa Women's University, Seoul, Korea
Julie Manning	Ritsumeikan Uji High School, Kyoto, Japan
Gloria McPherson	English Language Institute, Seneca College, Ontario, Canada
Mary E. Meloy Lara	John F. Kennedy Primary School, Puebla, Mexico
Young-in Moon	English Language and Literature Department, Seoul National University, Korea
Junil Oh	Pukyong National University, Pusan, Korea
Serdar Ozturk	Terraki Vakfi Okullarj, Istanbul, Turkey
Diana Pelyk	Ritsumeikan Asia Pacific University, Oita, Japan
Stephen Russell	Meiji Gakuin University, Tokyo, Japan
Consuelo Sañudo	Subsecretaria de Servicios Educativos para el Distrito Federal, Mexico
Robin Strickler	Kansai Gaidai University, Osaka, Japan
Liu Su-Fen	Mingchi Institute of Technology, Taipei, Taiwan
Cynthia Cheng-Fang Tsui	National Chengchi University, Taipei, Taiwan
Beatrice Vanni	University of Bahcesehir, Istanbul, Turkey
Kerry Vrabel	LaGuardia Community College, New York, U.S.A.
Aysen Yurdakul	Buyuk Kolej, Ankara, Turkey

Contents

Are You an ACTIVE Reader?

Before you use this book to develop your reading skills, take a minute to think about your reading habits, and your strengths and weaknesses when reading in English.

1. Do you enjoy reading in your native language?　　　☐ Yes　　　☐ No

2. How much time do you spend each day reading in your native language? _____

3. What types of material do you read in your native language?

    ☐ newspapers　　　☐ textbooks　　　☐ magazines

    ☐ poetry　　　☐ fiction　　　☐ nonfiction

    ☐ e-mails　　　☐ websites　　　☐ letters from friends or family

    ☐ Other: _____

4. Why do you read these materials?

    ☐ Pleasure　　　☐ I have to　　　☐ Both

5. Do you enjoy reading in English?　　　☐ Yes　　　☐ No

6. How much time do you spend each day reading in English? _____

7. What types of material do you read in English?

    ☐ newspapers　　　☐ textbooks　　　☐ magazines

    ☐ poetry　　　☐ fiction　　　☐ nonfiction

    ☐ e-mails　　　☐ websites　　　☐ letters from friends or family

    ☐ Other: _____

8. Why do you read these materials?

    ☐ Pleasure　　　☐ I have to　　　☐ Both

9. Assess your reading. Circle one of the two choices for each of the reading areas below.

a. speed	fast	slow	_____
b. comprehension	good	not so good	_____
c. vocabulary	good	not so good	_____
d. use of reading skills	good	not so good	_____

10. Which of the areas above would you most like to improve? Outside of class, look through the first unit of the book and, on the lines above, write down the section(s) of the unit that you think will help you improve each of the above areas. As you work through the book, pay attention to those areas that will help you to improve your reading skills.

Keeping Time

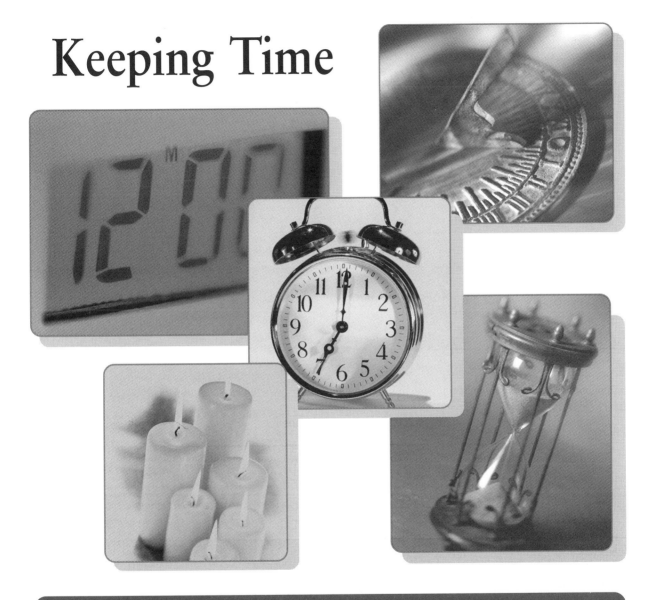

Getting Ready

Discuss the following questions with a partner.

1. *Do you know the names of all the objects in the pictures? Match the words below to the correct picture.*

   sundial   hourglass   alarm clock
   candles   digital clock

2. *How many clocks do you have in your home? Which rooms are they in?*
3. *How many watches do you own? Do you wear a watch every day? If not, why?*
4. *Do you think being punctual is important? Why?*

Before You Read:

Knowledge of Time

(A) How much do you know about the history of time-keeping? Read each statement and decide if it is true (*T*) or false (*F*).

		T	F
1.	Over the years, humans have used candles, water, and sand to keep track of time.		
2.	The sundial was one of the earliest instruments used to keep track of time.		
3.	Battery-powered clocks were invented in the twentieth century.		
4.	The first alarm clock was made using a candle and a nail.		
5.	Most clocks and watches are now powered by batteries that last for a few months.		
6.	Today, time is monitored around the world using powerful clocks.		

(B) The following words can all be found in the reading. What do you think each word means?

fascinated   reliable   coordinated   portable   equal

Reading Skill:

Predicting

> When we know what the topic of a reading is, we can use our 'internal' knowledge (what we already know about the topic) to predict the words, or the kind of information, we will read. Using this skill can help us to better understand what we will read about.

(A) Look at your answers from A, above. Now read the article to see if your predictions were correct.

What Time Is It? _____

How many clocks do you have in your home? In today's busy world, following schedules and being punctual[1] are a part of daily life. Humans have been fascinated by the concept of time for centuries, and expressions such as "Time is money," "Time marches on," and "Time
5 flies when you're having fun" show how important time, and being on time, is in many cultures.

Time, as we understand and measure it—with clocks and calendars, is a human invention.[2] The science of studying time, as well as the art of making instruments that measure time, is known as horology; clock and
10 watchmakers are called horologists. Different instruments have been used to keep track of time over the years—the sun, water, candles, sand, springs, electricity, and quartz[3]—all in an effort to count time in equal units. Sundials, or sun clocks, were used as early as 3500 B.C. and divided daylight time into equal hours. By looking at a shadow cast by
15 the sun over the dial in the center, people were able to get a general idea

of the time of day. Use of the sundial became very popular in certain parts of the world, and around 1500 B.C., the Egyptians even had portable sundials.

In Europe, in the fourteenth century, the hourglass was used. Time was measured by having a quantity of sand, water, or mercury[4] run from the upper to the lower part over a set period of time. Europeans also used candles to monitor time. Early alarm clocks were made by sticking a nail into the side of a candle. When the candle burnt down, the wax[5] holding the nail would melt, and the nail would fall into the tin[6] candleholder. The noise of the nail hitting the tin would wake the sleeper.

The first spring-powered clock was invented by Peter Henlein of Germany around 1510. The power for this clock came from a metal coil[7] inside called a mainspring. To operate the clock, a person would wind[8] the mainspring by turning a key. As the spring unwound, it moved the hands of the clock. This was a more accurate timepiece than any previously used, but there was a problem; as the mainspring unwound, the hands of the clock moved slower, and the clock lost time.

Seth Thomas from the United States patented[9] the mechanical wind-up alarm clock in 1876. This clock didn't only keep time, it also allowed a person to set a 'wake-up time' and would ring a bell at the time the sleeper had set for awakening.

Battery-powered clocks were first used in the 1840s, with electric and quartz-powered clocks coming into use in the early 1900s. With the invention of battery and electric-powered clocks, there was no longer the need to wind a mainspring. As a result, time-keeping became much more accurate.

Today, most clocks are powered by small batteries that can last for a few years. Timepieces are much more reliable as a result, and so is the science of horology. Around the world, time is now monitored by highly reliable atomic[10] clocks that are coordinated to produce a universal time standard. The world time system consists of around 270 atomic clocks, which are in about fifty laboratories[11] around the world,

55 making the science of keeping time an international effort.

For many busy people in the modern world, how they spend their time can be a subject of great interest and concern. As an ancient philosopher once said, "Time is the most valuable thing a person can spend."

---

¹ **punctual** arriving or leaving on time for something
² **invention** something that is created or made for the first time
³ **quartz** a clear mineral used in electronic equipment
⁴ **mercury** a silver-colored metal that can become liquid, used in batteries and thermometers
⁵ **wax** a solid, usually white or yellow substance that melts when heated, often used to make candles
⁶ **tin** a silver-colored metal often used to make food or drink containers
⁷ **coil** a piece of wire formed into tight circles—one on top of the other; a spring
⁸ **wind** to turn something around and around a number of times, usually to tighten it
⁹ **patent** to have the legal right to make and sell an invention for a certain number of years
¹⁰ **atomic** nuclear; a very powerful form of energy used to make electricity
¹¹ **laboratory** a place, usually a room or building, used for doing scientific tests

---

(B) Look again at your answers from Before You Read. How many did you get correct? Check your answers with a partner.

Reading Comprehension:
What Do You Remember?

How much do you remember from the reading? Choose the best answer to complete each statement. Compare your answers with a partner.

1. A person who makes watches and clocks is called a _____.
   a. horology   **b.** horologer   **c.** horologist

2. The sundial divided _____ into equal units of time.
   a. a full day   **b.** daytime   **c.** morning only

3. The _____ was used in _____ in the fourteenth century to keep track of time.
   a. sundial / Egypt   **b.** candle / Germany   **c.** hourglass / Europe

4. To use a spring-powered clock, you had to _____.
   a. wind a key   **b.** ring a bell   **c.** turn the hands

5. The first _____ clock was patented in the 1800s.
   a. spring-powered   **b.** mechanical alarm   **c.** electric

6. The problem with spring-powered clocks was that they _____.
   a. lost time   **b.** rang too loudly
   c. had hands that moved too quickly

7. Clocks powered by _____ now work together to monitor time in different countries.
   a. battery   **b.** quartz   **c.** nuclear energy

Vocabulary Comprehension: Odd Word Out

Ⓐ For each group, circle the word that does not belong. The words in *italics* are vocabulary items from the reading.

1. *fascinated*	interest	concern	bore
2. device	tool	clothing	*instrument*
3. even	*equal*	alike	different
4. *monitor*	ignore	*keep track of*	follow
5. mobile	fixed	moveable	*portable*
6. *reliable*	trustworthy	dependable	unstable
7. mistaken	incorrect	*accurate*	wrong
8. disordered	*coordinated*	matched	synchronized

Ⓑ Complete the sentences using the words in *italics* from A. Be sure to use the correct form of the word.

1. A day is divided into twenty-four _____ parts, called hours.

2. I don't think it's a good idea to drive my car from Chicago to New York. It's almost twenty years old and not very _____.

3. The great thing about having a laptop computer is that it's _____; I can take it with me anywhere!

4. The thermometer is an _____ commonly used by doctors to _____ temperature.

5. I saw a great show on TV last night about different types of calendars used around the world. The show really _____ me.

6. There must be over one hundred students in my biology class. I just don't know how the teacher _____ us all!

7. The newspaper said the movie started at 8:00, but that wasn't _____. I arrived at the theater at 7:30, and the movie had already started.

8. Class schedules in this school are _____ so that they all begin at 8:00 and stop for lunch at noon.

Vocabulary Skill:

Idioms Using
Time

In this chapter, you read the idiom 'on time,' meaning 'at exactly the right time.' An idiom, or expression, is a fixed group of words that has a special meaning. There are many idioms that are formed using the word 'time.' Sometimes it's possible to know the idiom's meaning by looking at the individual words, but not always. Learning some of the most common types of idioms can help you increase your vocabulary.

Ⓐ Following are some common idioms that use the word *time*. Match each idiom with its definition.

1. spend time _____
2. save time _____
3. waste time _____
4. kill time _____
5. make time _____

a. to schedule a specific amount of time to do something
b. to use time in a certain way
c. to do something because you have too much time
d. to use less time, or do something quickly so you have more time to do something else
e. to use time poorly

Ⓑ Complete the following sentences with one of the *time* idioms from A. Be sure to use the correct form of the verb in each idiom.

1. If we take the bus to school, it will take an hour. Let's take a taxi instead. It'll only take twenty minutes and we'll _____.
2. Dai tries to _____ every day to read something in English.
3. How do you like to _____ during summer vacation—working or relaxing?
4. The movie doesn't start for another hour. We can _____ until then by having coffee across the street.
5. Professor Morgan wants to talk to me after class. She thinks I'm _____ training for a professional football team instead of applying to college.

Ⓒ Take turns asking and answering the following questions with a partner.

1. Do you ever waste a lot of time?
2. Name one way that you can kill time while waiting for a bus.
3. How often do you make time to study in the evenings?
4. How do you usually spend time on the weekends?
5. What is something you can do to save time in the morning and arrive at school or work earlier?

Think About It Discuss the following questions with a partner.

1. *Can you name any other instruments that people use to keep track of time?*
2. *Is the time on your watch accurate right now? How about the clocks in your home or car? Do you ever move the time ahead slightly? Why?*
3. *In the reading, there is a proverb, or saying, "Time is money." What do you think this means? Do you have any other sayings about time in your country?*
4. *How do you usually spend your free time? Are you a busy person, or do you have a lot of free time?*

Chapter 2: Are You a Procrastinator?

Discuss the following questions with a partner.

1. Do you ever put off studying or doing assignments, or do you usually do things right away?

2. Look at the title of the reading. What do you understand by the word *procrastinator*?

3. Do you ever procrastinate? When? Why do you procrastinate?

4. The following words and phrases can all be found in the reading. What do you think they mean?

put off   chronic   priority
overwhelmed   anxiety   avoid

Time yourself as you read through the passage. Try to read as fluently as you can. Record your time in the Reading Rate Chart on page 202.

Are You a Procrastinator?

Following a schedule and doing things on time is extremely important in today's busy world. Using time effectively is a valuable skill that everyone must master. Catching a bus, getting to work or school on time, and even meeting friends requires managing time. Unfortunately, not everyone is very good at doing this. Many people are procrastinators; they put off doing things that they need to until it's too late.

5

We all procrastinate sometimes. Statistics show that 90 percent of university students will often put off studying for a test or writing an

By building your reading fluency you will be able to read faster in exams. Improve your reading fluency, and you'll probably improve your exam scores!

7

important paper until the night before. Twenty-five percent of university students can be defined as chronic procrastinators. This more serious form of procrastination can result in a student dropping out[1] of school. Students who persistently[2] delay doing their assignments get further and further behind in their studies. Before long, they feel completely overwhelmed. For the chronic procrastinator, often the only way to solve this problem is to quit school.

According to recent studies, there are three main reasons that students procrastinate. First, many have poor time-management skills and often try to do too much in too little time. In the end, these students often feel overwhelmed and will put off doing many things they need to. Another reason that students procrastinate is because they feel a subject is boring or because they have difficulty concentrating[3] on an assignment. These students will often avoid[4] doing something because they don't like it. A third reason that many students procrastinate is because they are very anxious about doing assignments well enough. These students often worry that their work will never be as good as it should be and fear failure of any kind. Unfortunately, trying to do everything perfectly can often cause these students to put off doing any work at all.

Do you recognize any of these signs in yourself? If so, you may want to do something about your tendency to procrastinate. The following five tips may be helpful. First, list the things in life that are important to you, then, list the reasons that you are at school or university. Look at the two lists and see where they match. Is there something you need to do in order to achieve a life goal? Second, choose realistic goals for yourself; don't try to do more than you can. Decide how hard you can work and what you can do.

Third, once you have identified[5] your goals, list them in order of priority. If you have three things to do, ask yourself "Which should I do first?" As you become more aware of what you need to do and when you need to do it, you will feel more in control and will be able to complete tasks on time. Fourth, budget your time[6] wisely. Create a schedule that allows adequate time for accomplishing[7] a goal; for example, your schedule should give you enough time to study for and pass a test, as well as time to relax. Finally, take the time to reward yourself. When you are alone in your apartment or room, tell yourself all the good things that you are doing to reach your goals. When you accomplish a goal, do something good for yourself like going to the movies or hanging out with friends.

55

If you believe that you are a chronic procrastinator, you should try to get help before it is too late. Talk to a counselor[8] or friend, and discuss the problem. If you are a mild[9] procrastinator, be sure to keep yourself motivated, but don't worry too much. Remember—we all procrastinate at times.

60

---

[1] **drop out (of)** to quit and leave a program or school course
[2] **persistently** constantly, continuously
[3] **concentrating** giving all of your attention to something; focusing on something
[4] **avoid** to try not to do something, to keep away from something or someone
[5] **identify** to name or recognize something
[6] **budget your time** an expression meaning to plan and organize your time so that you use it well
[7] **accomplishing** finishing something; achieving or reaching something
[8] **counselor** a person who gives professional help and advice
[9] **mild** not serious, minor

Reading Comprehension: How Much Do You Remember?

(A) Decide if the following statements about the reading are true (*T*) or false (*F*). If you choose false, correct the statement to make it true.

	T	F
1. A procrastinator will often know how to use his or her time effectively.		
2. Almost all university students are chronic procrastinators.		
3. Chronic procrastinators usually drop out of school.		
4. The reading lists three main reasons that students procrastinate: boredom, worry about failure, and trying to do too much.		
5. The reading lists four tips that can help students stop procrastinating.		
6. The tips for overcoming procrastination suggest that a person should make time to study and have fun.		
7. The reading says that chronic procrastinators should talk to a teacher.		

(B) Check your answers with a partner. Count how many you got correct—be honest! Then, fill in the Reading Comprehension Chart on page 202.

Vocabulary Comprehension:
Words in Context

A The words in *italics* are vocabulary items from the reading. Read each question or statement and choose the correct answer. Compare your answers with a partner.

1. Which might you *put off* doing?
   a. waking up in the morning
   b. visiting the dentist

2. A *chronic* cold is one that you might have for one _____.
   a. week
   b. month

3. Hiroko has *mastered* playing the violin. In other words, she _____ it very well.
   a. plays
   b. doesn't play

4. It's 9:00 and you are at home. Your plane leaves at 9:15. You probably _____ have *adequate* time to catch your flight.
   a. do
   b. don't

5. A person who has a *tendency* to gain weight easily _____ eat fatty foods.
   a. should
   b. should not

6. The teacher didn't explain the story very *effectively*. As a result, many students _____.
   a. were confused
   b. passed the test

7. Which might make you feel very *overwhelmed*?
   a. meeting classmates during a break
   b. doing three things at once

8. Raquel has to study for a test and write a paper. The paper is her *priority*. Which will she do first?
   a. study for the test
   b. write the paper

9. During _____, many students are usually very *anxious*.
   a. final exams
   b. summer vacation

B Now think of other examples using the vocabulary from A. Discuss your ideas with a partner.

1. Do you ever *put off* visiting the dentist or doctor? Why?
2. Have you ever had a *chronic* cold or other type of illness?
3. Talk about something that you have *mastered* doing.
4. Do you have *adequate* time to study? Sleep? Go out with friends? Why or why not?
5. Do you, or does anyone you know, have a *tendency* to gain weight easily?
6. Talk about something that you cannot do very *effectively*.
7. When was the last time you felt *overwhelmed*?
8. Finish this sentence: My *priority* for this week is to _____.
9. When you take exams, do you feel calm or *anxious*?

Vocabulary Skill:
Synonyms

> A synonym is a word that has the same or similar meaning as another word. One way of increasing your vocabulary is by learning synonyms.

Ⓐ Read the letter below and see how many synonyms you can find for each vocabulary item in the chart. Write your answers in the synonyms column.

Vocabulary	Synonyms
1. put off	postpone
2. drop out (of)	
3. anxious	
4. adequate	
5. chronic	

Dear Angela,

Help, I have a problem. My university roommate, Sharon, told me today that she is going to drop out of school! She says that she has put off doing work for every class and no longer has adequate time, or enough energy, to finish. She thinks her only choice is to quit. I know that she procrastinates, and that this was a persistent problem, but I didn't know it was so serious. Sharon was going to talk to a counselor today about this problem, but she also postponed that meeting! I know she is feeling very anxious, but I'm also worried she is making a huge mistake. How can I help her with this chronic problem? I don't want her to leave school.

Concerned Friend
Seattle

Ⓑ Now complete the reply using the synonyms from the chart. Be sure to use the correct form of the word.

Dear Concerned Friend,

I know that you are (1)_____ about Sharon, but if she really wants to (2)_____ school, you can't stop her. You say that Sharon (3)_____ doing assignments, and that this problem is (4)_____. Well, maybe she doesn't have (5)_____ interest in school right now. If Sharon (6)_____ university, and gets a job, she might actually be happier than if she stayed in school.

Angela

Ⓒ Compare your answers with a partner. Do you agree with Angela's advice? What other advice would you give?

What Do You Think?

Discuss the following questions with a partner.

1. *The reading lists three reasons that students procrastinate. Do any of these describe you?*
2. *The reading lists five tips that can help students stop procrastinating. Which tip do you think is the most helpful?*
3. *Do you know anyone who is a chronic procrastinator? Describe this person.*
4. *Talk to your partner about something you are putting off doing. Listen as your partner gives you some advice.*

Real Life Skill

Recognizing Common Time Abbreviations

In this chapter, you read the time abbreviation B.C. meaning 'Before Christ.' There are many time abbreviations like this in English that are both written as well as spoken. Many abbreviations come from Latin, for example, A.D. (Anno Domini), A.M. (Ante Meridiem), and P.M. (Post Meridiem). When spoken, each letter of the abbreviation is pronounced.

A Practice saying each abbreviation. Then, match each one with its correct meaning.

Abbreviation	Used to talk about...
1. B.C. •	• a. the time, set near London, that the rest of the world's times are compared to
2. A.D. •	• b. the hours of 12:00 noon to 11:59 at night
3. A.M. •	• c. the years before the birth of Christ, using the Gregorian, or solar, calendar
4. P.M. •	• d. the time from April–October when clocks are set one hour ahead in the U.S.
5. G.M.T. •	• e. the years after Christ's birth
6. D.S.T. •	• f. the hours of 12:00 midnight to 11:59 in the morning

Note: *G.M.T. = Greenwich Mean Time; D.S.T. = Daylight-Saving Time*

B Calculate the answers to the questions below using the information above. Then, share your answers with a partner.

1. A person born in 500 B.C. was born how many years ago? _____
2. If G.M.T. is 11:00 P.M., what time is G.M.T. + 3? _____
3. Los Angeles is G.M.T. - 8, and in L.A. it is now 8:00 A.M. What time is it in London? _____
4. When D.S.T. starts in the U.S., the clocks change from 2:00 A.M. to _____.
5. A person was born in 35 A.D. and died at the age of 75. What year did the person die? _____
6. Tokyo is G.M.T. + 9, and G.M.T. right now is 5:30 P.M. What time is it in Tokyo? What time is it in Los Angeles? _____

Love and Marriage

Getting Ready

Discuss the following questions with a partner.

1. *What is happening in the photos above? Make a list of words that you can use to describe each picture.*
2. *In which country do you think this event is taking place? Why?*
3. *When was the last time you went to a wedding? Whose wedding was it?*
4. *What are some of the things people do at weddings in your country?*

Before You Read:
Perfect Partners

(A) Read each statement and think about your own opinion. Circle *Agree* or *Disagree*.

1. If two people have different life goals, they can still have a good marriage.   Agree   Disagree

2. It's important to be able to share *all* of your feelings with your partner.   Agree   Disagree

3. If two people have different personalities, their marriage probably won't work.   Agree   Disagree

4. You should never marry someone who is selfish or unkind.   Agree   Disagree

5. It's okay to marry someone who has qualities you don't like. If you love the person, you will be able to change her or him.   Agree   Disagree

(B) The following words and phrases can all be found in the reading. How do you think they are related to the topic of the reading?

(head over heels)   (compatible)   (self-centered)

(spouse)   (admire)

Reading Skill:
Scanning

> When we need to read something to find certain information, we move our eyes very quickly across the text. When we 'scan' like this, we do not read every word or stop when we see a word we do not know; we read quickly and stop only to find the information we are looking for.

(A) Now scan the reading to find Agnes's views on the statements above. How do your opinions compare? Share your answers with a partner.

(B) Read the passage again, then answer the questions that follow.

Have I Found Ms. Right? _____

In this month's *Dear Agnes* column, Agnes gives some sound advice on choosing the perfect marriage partner.

> **Q: Dear Agnes,**
> I recently met a wonderful woman, and I have fallen
> 5 head over heels in love with her. I think she may be
> Ms. Right, but I don't know. I want to marry her,
> but how can I be sure she is my ideal[1] partner?
> **Yong-Il,**
> **Seoul, Korea**

10 **A: Dear Yong-Il,**
Choosing your life partner is a decision that requires very careful thought. Getting married is something you do not want to take lightly.[2] Divorce rates around the world are increasing every year, and in some countries they are now as high as 50 percent! If you don't want to end

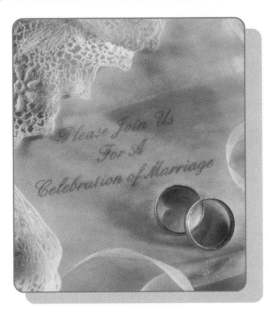

up[3] divorced and heart-broken, take my advice and follow these five rules to help you choose your perfect partner.

First of all, you and your partner should be compatible. You need to know that you share a common purpose in life. You and your partner should have similar goals and ambitions that you can work toward achieving throughout your married life. It will be difficult to keep your marriage together if your partner wants to stay at home and raise a large family, but you want to travel the world instead of having children. Find out what your intended[4] spouse's life goals are long before you tie the knot![5]

Next, ask yourself this question: Is my partner a person with whom I can share my innermost[6] thoughts and feelings? In other words, can you be completely honest and open with this person, or do you sometimes feel shy and uncomfortable telling her how you feel? If your situation is the former, then you have probably found your true love. If, however, it is the latter, take your time before you make plans to walk down the aisle[7] with this person.

Third, only marry someone who has qualities you admire. If you respect people who work hard, you should marry someone who is hard-working, not someone who is lazy or too easy-going.

Fourth, marry a person who is polite and kind to others; they will be polite and kind to you. In my experience, you can learn a lot about the true nature of a person by watching how he or she treats other people. A person who is kind and giving to family and friends will be kind and giving toward you. Someone who has good manners and is polite and respectful toward others will show you the same consideration.[8] Watch how your partner treats people she does not have to be nice to such as waiters, taxi drivers, or store clerks. Does your partner pay attention to how you and others feel, or does she have a self-centered nature?

Finally, when you enter into a relationship with someone, remember that you should not expect to change that person. If your partner has

55 qualities or faults[9] that you feel you cannot tolerate, then you probably shouldn't marry her. Marriage should be about accepting a person— with all their good and bad points—for life.

Finding your life partner is not always easy. Falling in love is a great feeling, so take time to enjoy all the emotions that go along with it. However, when you decide to marry, use your head *and* your heart to 60 think about things carefully. Spending the rest of your life with one person takes hard work and effort. Make sure that the person you marry is the right one for you.

---

[1] **ideal** best, perfect
[2] **take (something) lightly** to be very easy-going or unconcerned about something
[3] **end up** to arrive at a place or be in a situation finally; in the end
[4] **intended** planned or possible in the future
[5] **tie the knot** an informal way of saying 'get married'
[6] **innermost** deepest, most private and personal
[7] **walk down the aisle** an informal way of saying 'get married'
[8] **consideration** thoughtfulness, kindness, concern
[9] **fault** a weakness, an imperfection

Reading Comprehension:
What Do You Remember?

Decide if the following statements about the reading are true (*T*) or false (*F*). If you check (✔) false, correct the statement to make it true.

	T	F
1. Yong-Il isn't in love with his current girlfriend.		
2. Agnes suggests that a person shouldn't think too much or too long about getting married.		
3. In some countries, one in every two marriages ends in divorce.		
4. Agnes give four tips for choosing the right spouse and staying married.		
5. According to Agnes, a person who is rude to other people will probably be unkind and rude to his or her spouse.		
6. Agnes suggests that you should use your heart more than your head when you choose your life partner.		
7. According to Agnes, being married is not easy.		

A The words in *italics* are vocabulary items from the reading. Read each question or statement and choose the correct answer. Compare your answers with a partner.

1. Which of the following is *sound* advice?
   a. Get married before you finish university.
   b. Meet your partner's family before you marry.

2. Which pair is often not *compatible*?
   a. a dog and its puppy   **b.** a dog and a cat

3. Your father's *spouse* is your _____.
   a. wife   **b.** mother

4. You're going out with some friends. You can either go to a movie or a bar. You choose the *latter*. In other words, you want to go to the _____.
   a. movie   **b.** bar

5. You can choose to study English in Australia or the U.S. You choose the *former*. In other words you go to _____.
   a. Australia   **b.** the U.S.

6. Jin-Woo is *head over heels* in love with Eun-Hee. In other words, he loves her _____.
   a. a little   **b.** a lot.

7. Which person would most people *admire*?
   a. a doctor   **b.** a thief

8. A *self-centered* person typically thinks of _____ first.
   a. him- or herself   **b.** others

9. You can't *tolerate* noise from the street so you often _____ your window.
   a. open   **b.** close

B Now think of other examples using the vocabulary from A. Discuss your ideas with a partner.

1. Can you think of other *sound* advice to give someone who wants to marry?
2. Name another pair that isn't usually *compatible*.
3. What is your father's *spouse's* name?
4. Your friends want to go to a movie or a bar. Which would you prefer to do, the *former* or the *latter*?
5. Have you, or has someone you know, ever been *head over heels* in love?
6. Talk about someone that you *admire*.
7. Do you know anyone who is *self-centered*?
8. Finish this sentence: I can't *tolerate* _____ because
   _____.

Vocabulary Skill:
Antonyms

An antonym is a
word or phrase that
has the opposite
meaning of another
word or phrase.
One way of
increasing your
vocabulary is by
learning antonyms.

Ⓐ Complete the chart below using the antonyms in the box.

Vocabulary	Antonym
1. former	_____
2. self-centered	_____
3. tolerate	_____
4. incompatible	_____
5. married	_____
6. selfish	_____
7. easy-going	_____

compatible	can't stand	hard-working	generous
single	thoughtful	latter	

Ⓑ Complete the personal ad below using the antonyms from the chart in A.
Check your answers with a partner.

Are we (1) _____?
Hi! My name is Shiho. I'm 26 years old. I'm (2) _____—never
been married! I am a graduate student getting my master's degree in
psychology, and I'm very (3) _____. I want to meet a man
between the ages of 25–30. I (4) _____ cigarette smoking, so
please don't be a smoker. I don't like men who are self-centered or lazy,
but I DO like men who are (5) _____ and (6) _____. If
the (7) _____ describes you, please get in touch and let's meet
for coffee!

Ⓒ What kind of person wouldn't be a good match for Shiho? Use at least
four words or phrases from the chart in A to describe this person.

_____

_____

Think About It | Discuss the following questions with a partner.

1. *Do you think Agnes gives Yong-Il sound advice? Why or why not?*
2. *What qualities do you admire in a person? What qualities couldn't you tolerate in a person?*
3. *There is a saying that 'opposites attract.' Do you think that people who are different can also be compatible? Explain your answer.*
4. *Describe your ideal partner.*

Chapter 2: Wedding Customs

Discuss the following questions with a partner.

1. What is the couple in the picture about to do? What does this action symbolize?

2. At what age do men and women in your country usually get married?

3. What do you understand by the word *custom*? Give one example of a wedding custom from your country.

4. The following words can all be found in the reading. How do you think they are related to the topic of the reading?

traditional   *union*   *eternal*   *newlywed*   *veil*   *bouquet*

Time yourself as you read through the passage. Try to read as fluently as you can. Record your time in the Reading Rate Chart on page 202.

Reading Skill:
Developing Reading Fluency

> Developing reading fluency means improving your reading speed AND comprehension at the same time.

Wedding Customs _____

Marriage is an ancient religious and legal[1] practice celebrated around the world. Although the reasons that people marry are similar in many places, wedding customs vary from country to country.

In many countries, it is customary for the bride to wear a white dress as a symbol of purity. In traditional Japanese wedding ceremonies, the bride wears a white kimono. The tradition of wearing a special white dress only for the wedding ceremony started around 150 years ago.

5

Before that, most women could not afford to buy a dress that they would only wear once. Now, bridal dresses can be bought in a variety
10 of styles and fabrics,[2] and many brides have their dress specially made.

In different countries, colors other than white are worn by the bride or used as part of the wedding ceremony. In certain Asian countries and in the Middle East, red and orange are considered symbols of joy and happiness. In Chinese cultures, wedding invitations are usually red and
15 gold as these are colors symbolic of wealth and happiness. Wedding guests give gifts of money to the newlyweds in small red envelopes. Not all cultures, though, consider money a suitable gift. In many Western countries, especially the U.K., wedding guests give the bride and groom household items that they may need for their new home.

20 As part of many traditional wedding ceremonies, a bride wears a veil. Wearing a veil that covers the head and face is a tradition that is over 2,000 years old. Veils were originally worn as a sign of secrecy and modesty[3] and could only be removed by the husband after the ceremony. Today, many brides wear a veil, but only for decoration. In
25 some countries, a veil is placed between the bride and groom during the wedding ceremony so that they cannot see or touch each other until they are married.

In many cultures, couples exchange rings, usually made of gold or silver, during the marriage ceremony. The circular shape of the ring is
30 symbolic of the couple's eternal union. In Brazil, it is traditional to have the rings engraved,[4] with the bride's name on the groom's ring, and vice versa.[5] The wedding ring is usually worn on the third finger of the left or right hand, because it was once believed that a vein[6] ran directly from this finger to the heart.

35 Flowers play an important role in most weddings. Roses are said to be the flowers of love, and because roses usually bloom[7] in June, this has become the most popular month for weddings in many countries. Ivy is also used in wedding bouquets[8] because in early Greek times, it was thought to be a sign of everlasting love. After the wedding ceremony, it
40 is customary in many countries for the bride to throw her bouquet into a crowd of well wishers—usually her single female friends. It is said that the person who catches the bouquet will be the next one to marry. In Turkey, when a woman gets married, her female friends write their names on the inside of the shoes the bride will wear on her wedding
45 day. After the ceremony, if someone's name has rubbed off and cannot be read, it is said that this person will be the next to marry.

Many wedding customs that originated in one part of the world have been incorporated into marriage ceremonies in other countries. Today, couples can choose from many of the world's traditional customs to create their own special wedding ceremony.

50

> ¹ **legal** related to the law or rules made by the government
> ² **fabric** a type of cloth or material, e.g., cotton or silk, usually used to make clothing
> ³ **modesty** a type of behavior in which one tries to avoid attracting attention to oneself
> ⁴ **engrave** to cut a word or picture into wood, stone, or metal
> ⁵ **vice versa** the same, but also in reverse; the opposite is also true
> ⁶ **vein** a small tube in the body that carries blood to the heart
> ⁷ **bloom** to grow and open, usually used to talk about plants
> ⁸ **bouquet** a group of flowers put together, usually to be given as a gift or to be held in a ceremony

Reading Comprehension: How Much Do You Remember?

Ⓐ How much do you remember from the reading? Choose the best answer to complete each statement below.

1. The tradition of wearing a special dress only on one's wedding day is about _____ years old.
   a. 150   **b.** 2,000   **c.** 2,500

2. In some cultures, the bride wears a white dress as a traditional symbol of _____.
   a. modesty   **b.** purity   **c.** secrecy

3. In some Asian and Middle Eastern countries, which color is NOT traditionally part of a wedding ceremony?
   a. red   **b.** orange   **c.** blue

4. According to the reading, in which country would the wedding guests give the bride and groom money?
   a. Brazil   **b.** the U.K.   **c.** China

5. In many cultures, a wedding ring is worn on the third finger because people believed this finger _____.
   a. would bring good luck   **b.** is connected to the heart
   c. symbolizes eternity

6. There is a belief that the person who catches the bride's _____ will _____.
   a. shoe / meet his or her spouse at the wedding   **b.** veil / have good luck
   c. flowers / be the next to marry

7. In which country is it customary to write the bride and groom's names in the wedding rings?
   a. Greece   **b.** Brazil   **c.** Turkey

Ⓑ Check your answers with a partner. Count how many you got correct—be honest! Then fill in the Comprehension Rate Chart on page 202.

Vocabulary Comprehension: Odd Word Out

Ⓐ For each group, circle the word that does not belong. The words in *italics* are vocabulary items from the reading.

1. *custom*	tradition	change	the norm
2. cleanliness	*purity*	used	untouched
3. groom	boyfriend	bride	*newlywed*
4. customary	modern	*traditional*	usual
5. appropriate	proper	wrong	*suitable*
6. short-term	*eternal*	temporary	brief
7. ornament	plain	*decoration*	design
8. *union*	parting	separation	division
9. represent	*symbolize*	include	stand for

Ⓑ Complete the sentences using the words in *italics* from A. Be sure to use the correct form of the word.

1. Robert has a beautiful _____ hanging on his wall; it comes from Tahiti.

2. Jeans and a T-shirt aren't _____ clothes to wear to most weddings.

3. Neil and Sarah are _____; they just got married two weeks ago.

4. When Uk-Jin and Eun-Hwa got married, they first had a Western-style wedding, and later a _____ Korean wedding ceremony.

5. There is a wedding _____ in the U.S. that says a bride should wear 'something old, something new, something borrowed, and something blue' on her wedding day.

6. The tradition of marriage celebrates the _____ of two people into one family.

7. In different cultures, different colors are used to _____ wealth and happiness.

8. That movie was so long and boring, it seemed to last an _____ amount of time.

9. In some cultures, the lotus flower is considered a symbol of perfection and _____.

Vocabulary Skill:
Word Families

(A) Complete the chart with the noun, verb, and adjective forms of words you've learned in this chapter. Be careful—not every word will have all three. Look again at the reading to find related words, or use your dictionary to help you.

When you learn a new word in English, it is helpful to also learn words that are related to it. Learning the different parts of speech that form the word family can help you to expand your vocabulary.

Noun	Verb	Adjective
_____	symbolize	_____
custom	_____	decorative
_____	_____	_____
purity	_____	traditional
_____	suit	_____
_____	_____	eternal

(B) Now complete the paragraph below with the correct word from the chart. Be sure to use the correct form of the word.

Wedding Symbols and Superstitions

What will bring good luck to the bride and groom on their wedding day? Different cultures have different beliefs, but nearly all do something to wish the couple a long and happy marriage.

In Italy, it's (1)_____ for the wedding guests to tie a ribbon in front of the building where the couple will marry. This is a (2)_____ of the couple's (3)_____ bond of marriage. There is another (4)_____ in which the bride gives guests 'confetti,' which are small bags of candy-covered almonds. Confetti is a (5)_____ of fertility or the ability to have children.

In Korea, ducks and geese (6)_____ faithfulness because they stay together for life. Many years ago, when a man found a (7)_____ wife, he would often give her family a pair of geese. Today, a Korean wedding ceremony may include (8)_____ such as hand-painted ducks. These are a (9)_____ of the couple's promise to stay together.

In Japan, in addition to wearing a white kimono, many women were traditionally painted completely white. This was done as a (10)_____ to the gods that the woman was (11)_____. The woman also wore a heavy headpiece. On this were many beautiful (12)_____. People believed this headpiece could attract good luck to the couple.

What Do You Think?

Discuss the following questions with a partner.

1. *How many of the wedding traditions talked about in this chapter are customary in your country?*

2. *What is a suitable wedding present to give someone in your country?*

3. *Think of an interesting wedding custom that is common in your country and write a short paragraph about it. Try to use as many new words from this chapter as possible.*

4. *Describe your ideal wedding. What would it be like? Who would you invite? Where would it be?*

Real Life Skill

Invitations

People often send invitations by regular post or e-mail asking others to join them for a meal, a celebratory party, or a night out. Some words and phrases are typically found in invitations. Certain expressions are also used to accept or decline an invitation.

Ⓐ Look at the highlighted words in the invitation below. What do you think they mean?

> *You're **invited** to Tom and Amy's **engagement party**!*
>
> **The Blue Moon**
> *1453 South Mission Boulevard*
>
> *Saturday, May 17   7:00 P.M. – **late***
> ***Cocktails** and **hors d'oeuvres** will be served*
> ***Dress code:** Casual*
> ***RSVP:** No later than May 1*

Ⓑ Read the two replies. Who is going to the party? Who isn't? Underline the words and phrases that helped you decide.

> May 1
>
> Tom and Amy,
> Thanks for the invitation; the party sounds like a lot of fun. I'm afraid I won't be able to make it though. I'm going to be out of town that weekend. Congratulations on the marriage plans!
>
> Toshi

> April 25
>
> Tom and Amy,
> Thanks for the invitation; the party sounds like a lot of fun. Kim and I are coming. Looking forward to seeing you!
>
> Rita

Ⓒ You are invited to Tom and Amy's party. Using the expressions you've learned, send a reply accepting or declining the invitation.

_____

_____

_____

What's Stressing You Out?

Getting Ready

Take the survey below. Then, share your answers with a partner.

Are You Stressed Out?

Choose the answer that best describes you.

1. Usually, I feel like I have _____ work to do.

   a. too much   **b.** the right amount of   **c.** very little

2. At night, I usually get into bed and _____.

   a. stay awake worrying   **b.** relax then fall asleep   **c.** go to sleep right away

3. New and unfamiliar situations make me feel _____.

   a. very worried   **b.** a little nervous   **c.** kind of bored

4. When I miss the bus, I usually feel _____.

   a. very angry   **b.** a little angry   **c.** unhappy but not angry

5. You have to write a paper for a class. It's due in one month. When will you start?

   a. the day before it is due   **b.** a week or two before it is due

   c. immediately

6. When I feel worried or anxious, I usually _____.

   a. drink, eat, or smoke   **b.** exercise or talk with others

   c. try not to think about it; it's not important

Points: a=3   b=2   c=1

15–18 points:
You probably have a lot of stress in your life. You need to find ways to relax and control the stress; don't let it control you.

8–14 points:
You have a healthy amount of stress in your life—enough to keep you motivated, but not stressed out all the time.

7 or fewer points:
You might have a tendency to be a little too relaxed. Remember, a little stress can be a good thing!

Before You Read:
Talk about Stress

Discuss the following questions with a partner.

1. Do your results from the survey in Getting Ready describe you? Why or why not?
2. List three things that can cause stress.
3. When was the last time you felt stressed out? What caused you to feel stressed?
4. The following words and phrases can all be found in the reading. What do you think they mean?

oversleep   deadline   cope with

due   hand in

Reading Skill:
Skimming for the Main Idea

> 'Skimming' is one way to look for the main ideas in a reading. When we skim, we read over parts of the text very quickly. We don't need to read every word, or look up words we don't understand; we just need to get a general idea of what the reading is about.

(A) Skim the passage quickly. Read only the *title*, the *first and last paragraphs*, and the *first sentence of each of the other paragraphs*. Don't worry about words you don't know. Then, complete the sentence.

This reading is mainly about _____.

1. ways that university students can control stress in their lives
2. ways that stress can improve the lives of university students
3. situations that can cause stress for university students

Study Stress _____

In this issue of *Maintaining Good Health*, Dr. Benjamin O'Dell, a stress therapist,[1] interviews a university student—Fumiko Yamada. They discuss the ways in which a university student's life can be stressful.

Dr. O'Dell: How stressful is the life of a university student?

5 **Fumiko:** Well, in my opinion, it's pretty stressful. Like most of my friends, in addition to studying at university, I work part-time. Spending time at work means that I have less time to prepare assignments or study for tests, so my stress levels increase. My friends and I often feel completely overwhelmed by the amount of work we have to do. It feels

10 like there are not enough hours in the day to get everything done.

Dr. O'Dell: Can you give me some examples?

Fumiko: Sure, that's easy. At the end of last term, just before winter break, I had a lot of papers due. The restaurant I work at was very busy, so I was working more hours than usual, and besides,[2] I needed

15 the money. I overslept one morning and was late for an important meeting with one of my professors. Later that day, I realized that I had a paper due the following day. I had completely forgotten about it, and

I hadn't started working on it! That same afternoon I was going to work on another assignment that was also due that week. On top of[3] everything else, I had to work at the restaurant that night. I almost cried when I realized how much work I had to do!

Dr. O'Dell: It sounds like that was a very stressful day. How did you cope with everything?
Fumiko: Well, a friend helped me to prioritize[4] things. First, I phoned the restaurant and asked to start work later than usual. Then, I went to see my professor, to talk to him about the paper due the next day—the one I hadn't started. When I asked him for an extension,[5] he became quite angry. He had given us weeks to complete the assignment, and most of the class had already handed in their papers—before the deadline! He agreed that I could submit[6] the paper late, but said that he would deduct[7] points for lateness.

Dr. O'Dell: How did that make you feel?
Fumiko: I was really shocked. I thought it was unfair at first, but it made me realize just how disorganized I am, and how much I procrastinate. This experience taught me a lesson.

Dr. O'Dell: Did you finish the other assignments on time?
Fumiko: Yes, I did, but I got really low grades because I did the work in such a hurry. By the end of the term, I was so stressed out from worrying about my assignments that I got sick. I spent most of the holidays in bed!

Dr. O'Dell: So, you think that being stressed out made you sick?
Fumiko: Definitely. I read somewhere that stress can cause health problems. Whenever I'm late for class, I get nervous and I feel sick. Also, if I spend too much time thinking about how much work I have to do, I get a headache.

Dr. O'Dell: I'm glad you've made the connection between stress and health. Many people don't realize that a lot of their health problems can be avoided by having less stress in their lives. I think that what you need to work on, Fumiko, is managing your time and therefore, the
50 level of stress you experience in your life.

In the next issue of *Maintaining Good Health*, Dr. O'Dell and Fumiko Yamada will talk about how she can control stress in her busy life.

---

¹ **therapist** a person who treats illnesses of the mind or body
² **besides** in addition, also
³ **on top of** in addition to, as well as
⁴ **prioritize** to organize things by order of importance
⁵ **extension** more time to do something
⁶ **submit** to give, to hand in
⁷ **deduct** to subtract or take away something

B Now read the interview again, then answer the questions that follow.

Reading Comprehension: What Do You Remember?

Decide if the following statements about the reading are true (*T*) or false (*F*). If you check (✔) false, correct the statement to make it true.

	T	F
1. Benjamin O'Dell is a teacher who helps people enter university.		
2. Fumiko believes that the life of a university student is very stressful.		
3. Fumiko goes to school and also has a full-time job.		
4. Fumiko visited one of her professors to give him a late paper.		
5. At the end of the term, Fumiko was happy with her grades.		
6. Fumiko was sick for most of the winter holiday.		
7. Dr. O'Dell believes that stress can make a person ill.		

Vocabulary Comprehension: Word Definitions

⒜ What part of speech is each of the following vocabulary items from the reading? Write *noun, verb,* or *adjective* in the chart below.

⒝ For each word or phrase, write the letter of the definition in the chart.

Vocabulary	Part of Speech	Definition
1. maintaining	noun	d
2. stress		
3. due		
4. oversleep		
5. cope (with)		
6. hand in		
7. stressed out		
8. deadline		
9. connection		

a. the time or day that something must be finished

b. great worry and anxiety, usually caused by a difficult situation

c. to give or deliver something to someone else

d. keeping something in a certain way, caring for something so that it doesn't change

e. expected or scheduled to happen at a specific time, e.g., paying a bill

f. to handle, manage, or deal with something successfully

g. to sleep longer than planned, to wake up late

h. very worried or anxious

i. the way in which one thing is related to or associated with another thing

⒞ Complete the sentences below using the vocabulary items from B. Be sure to use the correct form of the word.

1. Naoki: When is the _____ for our English paper?
Etsuko: I think it's _____ on March 3.

2. _____ a healthy diet while going to school and working can be hard to do.

3. Paula: What's wrong, Carol? You look really _____.
Carol: I am. I _____ this morning and missed a final exam!

4. Thomas couldn't _____ all the work in his chemistry class, and so he dropped it.

5. Research suggests that there is a _____ between eating a good breakfast and paying attention in class.

6. When you finish the exam, please _____ your paper to the assistant.

7. The _____ of studying for her university entrance exam has made Li-Lin ill. She's in bed with a terrible stomachache.

Vocabulary Skill:

The Prefixes *over-* and *under-*

In this chapter, you learned the verb 'oversleep,' meaning 'to sleep too much.' This word is formed by adding the prefix 'over-' to the verb 'sleep.' The prefix 'over-' can mean 'too much' or 'more;' the prefix 'under-' can mean 'too little' or 'beneath.'

A What do you think the following words mean? Use each word to complete the sentences below.

overcook	overcome	overdue	overtime
understaffed	underground	underwear	

1. We need to pay these bills today. They are two weeks _____.

2. Beneath the city of London, there are many _____ passages that were used during World War II.

3. Four teachers have left the university, so now the English department is _____.

4. The restaurant was very busy this week, so Fumiko had to work ten hours _____.

5. Don't _____ the chicken or it will be too dry to eat.

6. If you want to stay really warm during the winter, I suggest wearing wool clothes and silk _____.

7. One way to _____ the desire to smoke is to chew gum.

B Now use either *over-* or *under-* to complete the sentences below. Check your answers with a partner.

1. If you let stress _____power you, you'll get so nervous you won't be able to do anything.

2. Jorge is 183 centimeters tall, but he's several kilos _____weight. He only weighs 70 kg.

3. Poor Yuko is terribly _____worked. She should only work from 9:00–5:00, but most days she works until 8:00 or 9:00.

4. Simon poured the tea into the cup too quickly, and it _____flowed onto the table.

5. Carla is _____paid. She makes $4 per hour, but she really should make more money.

6. What is the capital of Italy? Please _____line the correct answer: Rome, Milan, Venice.

Think About It **Discuss the following questions with a partner.**

1. *Do you think that a university student's life is stressful? Give an example.*

2. *Have you ever handed in a paper or homework after the deadline? How did you feel?*

3. *Do you believe that there is a connection between stress and health? Give some examples.*

4. *What are some ways that people can cope with stress?*

Discuss the following questions with a partner.

1. Describe a typical day for you. Do you try to organize your time or do you just let things happen?

2. How often do you stay up late working or studying?

3. Look at the title of the reading. What do you think this passage is about?

4. The following words and phrases can all be found in the reading. What do you think they mean?

remedy   self-discipline   strategically   will power   eliminate

Time yourself as you read through the passage. Try to read as fluently as you can. Record your time in the Reading Rate Chart on page 202.

Reading Skill:
Developing
Reading
Fluency

Managing Stress ——————————————————

In the last issue of *Maintaining Good Health*, we featured an interview with stress therapist Dr. Benjamin O'Dell and university student Fumiko Yamada. They talked about how stress can affect the lives of university students. In this issue, Dr. O'Dell and Fumiko share ideas on how to cope with and control stress.   5

> *Reading fluently can help you increase your comprehension. Focus on what you can comprehend, not on what you can't.*

Dr. O'Dell: Fumiko, let's recap[1] by talking about the issues[2] that have caused stress in your life.
Fumiko: Okay. Well, handing in my assignments late has been the biggest source of stress. Being late for classes has been a problem, too.

Dr. O'Dell: Now that you've identified these problems, what do you   10
think is causing them?

Fumiko: I think there are two main causes. First, I'm very disorganized; that is, I just don't manage my time very well. Second, I procrastinate. I often wait until it's too late to start writing or studying. As for being late for class so often, well, because I'm behind with my studies, I stay up[3] late trying to complete assignments or catch up on my reading. Often, I don't get to bed until 3 A.M., and then I oversleep in the morning.

Dr. O'Dell: What do you think is the best way to remedy the situation?

Fumiko: First, I need to be more organized, and budget my time better. This semester, I've created a timetable for myself; I've scheduled my entire day—from morning until evening. I really think this will help me a lot. Second, I need to think more about my priorities in life; right now, my studies are more important than my part-time job.

Dr. O'Dell: Excellent. What do you plan to do about your procrastination and chronic lateness to class?

Fumiko: Well, I think that this semester, by planning my time more strategically, I can overcome my tendency to procrastinate. If I follow my schedule, I'll spend less time watching TV and hanging out[4] at the coffee shop with my friends. I'll get more done during the day, which means I won't have to stay up all night.

Dr. O'Dell: It sounds challenging.[5] Do you think you'll be able to make such a big lifestyle[6] change?

Fumiko: It's going to take a lot of will power and self-discipline, but I know that my life will be better. I'll complete my assignments on time; I won't be tired in the mornings. In the end, I'll be less stressed out, and I'll have fewer health problems.

Dr. O'Dell: What about your job? How do you intend to manage all of this and continue to work?

Fumiko: As I mentioned earlier, I need to rethink my priorities and put my studies first. That means my job comes second. I don't want to quit my job, but I do need to work fewer hours. This semester, I'm only going to work on weekends—Saturday nights and Sunday afternoons. I won't be able to go out with my friends on Saturday nights, but I'll save more money. Also, if I get behind[7] with my studies during the week, I will have time to catch up because I won't be working so much.

Dr. O'Dell: Well, Fumiko, it sounds like you have everything under control.[8] How is your new schedule working?

Fumiko: I started following it this week, and so far, it's been fine. My life isn't completely stress-free now, I mean, I still feel stressed out if I miss the bus and get to school a little late, but things are much less stressful than they were last semester.

Dr. O'Dell: That's good, and remember, it's not really possible to eliminate stress from our lives completely. The important thing is not to let stress overpower you. Understanding what causes your stress and finding ways to solve the problem are the best things to do.

55

---

¹ **recap** to repeat the main points or ideas
² **issue** an important point; a problem
³ **stay up** to remain, or continue to be, awake
⁴ **hanging out** spending time in a place or with other people
⁵ **challenging** demanding, difficult, not easy
⁶ **lifestyle** a way of living one's life
⁷ **get behind** to become late or go more slowly than others
⁸ **under control** organized, working properly, controlled well

---

Reading Comprehension: How Much Do You Remember?

Ⓐ Choose the best answer for each question or statement below. Try not to look back at the reading for the answers.

1. In this interview, Dr. O'Dell and Fumiko are mainly talking about _____ stress.
   a. creating
   b. controlling
   c. eliminating

2. According to this interview, which is NOT a cause of stress in Fumiko's life?
   a. getting to work late
   b. arriving to classes late
   c. handing in school work late

3. Fumiko often _____ in the morning because _____.
   a. wakes up early / she has to finish her homework
   b. begins studying at 3 A.M. / she can't sleep
   c. gets up late / she does school work until late at night

4. Fumiko plans to _____ to lower the stress in her life this semester.
   a. organize and schedule her day
   b. put her studies before her job
   c. do both a and b

5. Fumiko says that making a change to her lifestyle will _____.
   a. be quite easy
   b. take patience and hard work
   c. not happen for a while

6. Fumiko thinks that her life this semester is _____.
   a. extremely stressful
   b. still a little stressful
   c. totally stress-free

7. In Dr. O'Dell's opinion, _____.
   a. you can't remove stress completely from your life; you have to learn to control it
   b. stress can overpower you, so you should try to eliminate it from your life
   c. you have to control stress by eliminating it from your life

(B) Check your answers with a partner. Count how many you got correct—be honest! Then fill in the Reading Comprehension Chart on page 202.

Vocabulary Comprehension: Words in Context

(A) The words in *italics* are vocabulary items from the reading. Read each question or statement and choose the correct answer. Compare your answers with a partner.

1. You have been sick for two days and have missed an important lecture. How can you *catch up* on your schoolwork?

   a. by visiting the doctor   **b.** by borrowing a classmate's notes

2. You had a fight with a good friend. You can *remedy* the situation by calling your friend and _____.

   a. apologizing   **b.** shouting at him

3. If you *eliminate* junk food from your diet, you _____ it.

   a. don't eat   **b.** eat more of

4. You are in a café where many people are smoking. The smell finally *overpowers* you and you _____.

   a. begin coughing   **b.** order some coffee

5. If you *intend* to meet friends, you _____ see them.

   a. don't want to   **b.** plan to

6. You have a lot of things to do tomorrow. If you use your time *strategically*, you _____ be able to do everything.

   a. will   **b.** won't

7. If you *overcome* a desire to skip class, you _____ to class.

   a. go   **b.** don't go

8. It's hard to quit smoking, but people with a lot of *will power* and *self-discipline* are often _____ to do it.

   a. able   **b.** unable

(B) Now think of other examples using the vocabulary from A. Discuss your ideas with a partner.

1. What is another way that you can *catch up* on your schoolwork?

2. If you have a fight with a friend, how else can you *remedy* the situation?

3. Why might someone *eliminate* junk food from his or her diet?

4. Have you ever been *overpowered* by the smell of something?

5. Do you *intend* to meet friends after class today?

6. When you have many things to do, do you use your time *strategically*?

7. When did you last *overcome* the desire to do something? What was it?

8. What else might take a lot of *will power* and *self-discipline* to do?

Ⓐ Read the example. Then, complete the sentences with *how, when,* or *where.*

> *Example:* Ayumi answered the question *correctly. Correctly*
> tells ____**how**____ she answered the question.

1. William is a *very* nice man. *Very* tells _____ nice William is.

2. Paul went to a movie *yesterday* with some friends. *Yesterday* tells _____ Paul went to the movies.

3. Ms. Tan isn't *here*. She went *outside. Here* and *outside* tell _____ Ms. Tan is.

4. We talked *before* our English class this morning. *Before* tells _____ we talked.

Ⓑ Underline the adverbs in the following paragraph. Check your answers with a partner.

> We all know that a little bit of stress can be a good thing, as it can motivate a person to take action—to do better in school, get to work earlier, or contact a friend. A lot of stress, though, can seriously affect one's mental and physical health and can prevent a person from doing things effectively. The causes of negative stress are everywhere. Many people know that a job, schoolwork, or lifestyle can cause negative stress levels to increase dramatically, but very few are aware that certain kinds of food and drink, if consumed regularly, can lead to higher levels of stress.

Ⓒ Now write two sentences using at least two of the adverbs from B.

1. _____

2. _____

Vocabulary Skill:
Identifying Adverbs

> In this chapter you learned the adverb 'strategically.' An adverb is a word that explains how, when, or where something happens or is done. An adverb describes a verb, an adjective, or another adverb.

What Do You Think?

Discuss the following questions with a partner.

1. *Do you have a lot of will power and self-discipline? Explain using examples.*

2. *Do you think that stress can be good in some ways?*

3. *What is something you want to eliminate from your life? How do you intend to do it?*

Real Life Skill

Dictionary Usage: Parts of Speech

When you learn new words in English, it is also helpful to learn their parts of speech so that you understand how to use them in sentences. You can use your dictionary to learn a word's part of speech, as well as related word forms (e.g., stress, stressed, stressful).

Ⓐ Below are some of the parts of speech that appear in dictionaries. Work with a partner to complete the Description column.

Part of Speech	Example	Description
noun (n)	Tom has a lot of **stress** in his life.	*a person, place, or thing*
verb (v)	Jessica **studies** Spanish.	
adjective (adj)	Fumiko had a **stressful** day. She felt **stressed out**.	
adverb (adv)	He read the paper **very carefully**.	
phrasal verb (phr v)	Hiromi **handed in** her paper.	
conjunction (conj)	Where are my hat **and** coat?	*joins two or more words, sentences, or ideas*
preposition (prep)	The cup is **on** the table.	*describes time and location*
	Your name is **after** mine on the list.	*makes a comparison between things*

Ⓑ Read each sentence. For each italicized word, write the correct part of speech. Use your dictionary to help you.

1. John sure drives *fast*. It makes me nervous!   *adverb*
2. I'm going to *fast* today; I won't eat anything until tomorrow. _____
3. Sandra is a really *fast* learner. _____
4. I've *put off* visiting the dentist for two years. _____
5. Excuse me, I think I am *before* you in line. _____
6. You've met Junko *before*, haven't you? _____
7. I need to repay my student *loan* this year. _____
8. Could you *loan* me $10 until tomorrow? _____
9. I don't have $10. *However*, I do have $5. _____

Ⓒ Complete each sentence with the correct word. Use your dictionary to help you. Explain your answers to a partner.

1. Young-ju looks really (different / difference / differ / differently) with short hair.
2. Richard (looked / looked up) the word in the dictionary to find its meaning.
3. Daisuke is older (then / than) Kenji.
4. Chan's (strategy / strategic / strategically) for passing a test is simple; he studies every day for an hour.
5. Excuse me, but could you please speak more (slow / slowness / slowly)?
6. The wire is (connection / connected / connect) to the back of the computer.

Amazing Animals

Getting Ready

Discuss the following questions with a partner.

1. *Can you name the animals in the photos above? Do you know where their natural habitats are?*
2. *What do you think these animals have in common?*
3. *What do you understand by the word 'endangered'?*
4. *Can you name any other animals that are endangered?*

Before You Read:

The Threat of Pollution

Ⓐ Read the sentences below. Which sentence helped you to understand the meaning of the word *threaten*? Explain your answer to a partner.

- Pollution *threatens*.
- Pollution *threatens* many plants and animals.
- Pollution *threatens* many plants and animals, and they are now in danger of dying.

Ⓑ Find each italicized word below in the reading passage. Read the sentence the word is in and some of the surrounding sentences. Then choose the best definition.

1. In line 22, the word *extinct* means

    a. very dangerous   **b.** no longer living   **c.** nearly dead

2. In line 30, the word *factors* means

    a. people with opinions   **b.** two or more numbers   **c.** facts that are possible

3. In line 44, the word *exotic* means

    a. foreign   **b.** local   **c.** expensive

4. In line 53, the word *ensure* means to be

    a. unsure   **b.** possible   **c.** certain

5. In line 61, the word *preserve* means to

    a. destroy   **b.** protect   **c.** create

Reading Skill:

Identifying Meaning from Context

> *To guess the meaning of an important but unfamiliar word in a passage, try the following strategy: First, think about how the new word is related to the topic of the reading. Second, notice the word's part of speech. Third, look at the words around the new word for synonyms, antonyms, or a definition of the word.*

Ⓐ Read the passage below. Pay attention to the words *estimated, exploitation, dying out, vulnerable, destruction,* and *intentionally.* Can you understand the meaning of these words?

Endangered Species _____

Several years ago, scientists estimated that over 1.5 million species[1] of animals and plants exist on earth. More recent estimates have increased that number to about 30 million. However, pollution, deforestation,[2] and exploitation of animals and plants now threaten many species. In
5 the U.S. alone, over 700 species of plants, and almost 500 species of animals, are listed as threatened or endangered, and are in danger of dying out.

The National Wildlife Federation places animal and plant species that are in danger of dying out into three categories. A *vulnerable species* is
10 in danger because its numbers are low or declining. The Mexican long-tongued bat and the lowland leopard frog are examples of vulnerable species. A *threatened species* is in danger because its habitat[3] is in

trouble. If the problem is not solved, this species will become endangered. The eastern indigo snake and the red kangaroo are examples of threatened species. An *endangered species* is in immediate danger of dying out completely, or becoming extinct. Its numbers are low and it needs protection in order to survive. There are more than 1,000 endangered animal species worldwide; the Siberian tiger and the snow leopard are two examples. The National Wildlife Federation also has a category for species that are extinct, or no longer living. Dinosaurs are probably the most famous example of an extinct species.

There are many factors that can cause an animal or plant species to become endangered. The main cause of species endangerment is humanity's destruction of both aquatic[4] and terrestrial[5] habitats. Deforestation and soil, air, and water pollution can all destroy a habitat. This can then cause a large number of animals or plants to die. Another cause of endangerment is exploitation of animals. Uncontrolled hunting[6] of whales in the last century, for example, caused many whale species to become endangered. A third cause of endangerment is the demand for animal parts for use in certain foods or medicines.

Introducing a non-native species to an environment can also cause species endangerment. A native species is one that develops naturally in a particular geographic[7] area, and has done so for a long time. A non-native species might be introduced into a new environment by humans, either intentionally or by accident. Other natural causes, such as changes in the weather, can also introduce an exotic species to a new environment. This exotic species may not be able to live with the native species, and the result may be the destruction of the native species or its natural habitat.

Many people do not worry greatly about species endangerment. However, it is important to remember that many life-saving medicines are created from certain plants or animals. The purple foxglove plant is, for example, the main source of the drug digitalis. Without this drug, over 3 million people in the U.S. would die every year within seventy-two hours of suffering a heart attack. To ensure that we have a long-

term supply of digitalis well into the future, we must make sure that the
55 purple foxglove and its habitat do not become endangered or extinct.

Societies such as the World Wildlife Fund, and the National Wildlife
Federation, try to raise awareness[8] of threatened animals and plants.
These organizations work with government agencies to save and
decrease the numbers of threatened or endangered species, and to make
60 new laws that will protect these species. Many of these plans work, but
some do not. Public awareness of this issue is important. To preserve
the quality of our lives, and the lives of future generations, we must
also protect plant and animal species now, and in the future.

---

[1] **species** a group of animals, plants, or insects that share common characteristics, and can breed together
[2] **deforestation** cutting down a large number of trees
[3] **habitat** the natural home or environment of an animal or plant
[4] **aquatic** related to bodies of water, e.g., rivers, oceans, seas
[5] **terrestrial** related to land
[6] **hunting** chasing and killing an animal for food or sport
[7] **geographic** related to the location of a piece of land or body of water
[8] **raise awareness** to increase people's understanding of something

---

B Read the passage again, then answer the questions that follow.

Reading Comprehension: What Do You Remember?

Decide if the following statements about the reading are true (*T*) or false (*F*). If you check (✔) false, correct the statement to make it true.

	T	F
1. Scientists believe that there are now 1.5 million species on earth.		
2. There are over 1,000 plant and animal species that are endangered.		
3. According to the National Wildlife Federation, a vulnerable species is one whose environment is in danger.		
4. According to the National Wildlife Federation, an endangered species is one that no longer exists.		
5. Today, most species become endangered because people hunt them.		
6. Introducing a foreign species into the natural habitat of another species can be dangerous.		
7. It is important to protect animal and plant life because we need them to create many important medicines.		

Ⓐ For each group, circle the word that does not belong. The words in *italics* are vocabulary items from the reading.

1. *estimate*	guess	assume	know
2. *threaten*	endanger	make safe	risk
3. helpless	*vulnerable*	weak	strong
4. preservation	protection	safety	*destruction*
5. nonexistent	dead	*extinct*	living
6. care	*exploitation*	abuse	mistreatment
7. *die out*	disappear	exist	become extinct
8. fact	training	*factor*	piece of information
9. on purpose	by accident	*intentionally*	knowingly

Ⓑ Complete the sentences below using the words in *italics* from A. Be sure to use the correct form of the word.

1. If we aren't careful, the giant panda will soon be completely _____.

2. I don't know the exact number, but I _____ that fifty people are coming to the meeting.

3. Many scientists believe that dinosaurs _____ over sixty million years ago.

4. Before you get a dog, there are two _____ to consider; are you allowed to have a pet in your apartment, and how much will the pet cost?

5. At first, I thought the man hit my car by accident, but then I realized he did it _____.

6. There is a worldwide effort to stop the _____ of the Brazilian rainforests.

7. Many countries have work and labor laws that prevent the _____ of children.

8. The man _____ to kill the woman unless she gave him all her money.

9. Young children need an adult to watch them because they are often helpless and can be very _____.

Vocabulary Skill:

Prefixes *ex-*, *en-*, and *em-*

In this chapter, you read the word 'exotic.' This word begins with the prefix 'ex-,' meaning 'out of' or 'from within.' You also read the word 'endangered,' which begins with the prefix 'en-,' meaning '(to put) into' or 'to cover.' When 'en-' comes before b or p, it changes to 'em-.'

Ⓐ What do you think the following words mean? Use them to complete the sentences below.

enclose   extend   exterior

embark   embrace

1. Do you see that sign over there that says "_____"? We get on the ship there.

2. After the car accident, Mark had to wear a cast and was unable to _____ his arm.

3. In some countries, people _____ and kiss each other on both cheeks when they meet.

4. When you mail the phone bill today, don't forget to _____ the payment in the envelope.

5. This building's _____ hasn't been painted in years and it looks terrible.

Ⓑ Now use *em-*, *en-*, or *ex-* to complete the words in the sentences below. Check your answers with a partner.

1. When Arthur gave Jill a new car, she _____pressed her thanks by hugging him.

2. Thirty minutes after the fire started, the building was completely _____veloped in flames.

3. The bullet is _____bedded in the door, and the police can't seem to remove it.

4. Sylvie works for a company that _____ports wine from France to Japan.

5. Rupert took out a knife and _____graved his name in the park bench.

Think About It   Discuss the following questions with a partner.

1. *Dinosaurs are extinct animals. Can you name other animals that are extinct? Why did these animals die out?*

2. *The National Wildlife Federation is an organization that protects endangered species. Do you know any other organizations or people that do this?*

3. *Do you think that sports such as fishing, bullfighting, or deer hunting are a kind of animal exploitation? Why or why not?*

4. *Create a poster that tells people about an endangered species. In the poster, give the following information: an estimate of the number of individuals of the species that are still alive; factors causing the species to die out; what people can do to prevent the species from becoming extinct.*

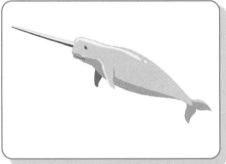

Discuss the following questions with a partner.

1. Look at the illustrations above. Can you name the animals? Which are real? Which exist only in mythology?

2. In what way do you think the animals in pictures one and two are related?

3. Look at the title of the reading. Which animals do you think you will read about?

4. The following words can all be found in the reading. How do you think they are related to the topic of the reading?

myth *fairy tale* *sacred*

mystical *virtue* *ancestor*

Time yourself as you read through the passage. Try to read as fluently as you can. Record your time in the Reading Rate Chart on page 202.

Animals in Mythology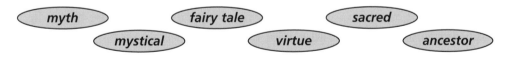

Reading Skill:
Developing
Reading
Fluency

Throughout history, stories have been written and told about different animals; many of these stories come from superstition[1] or popular myths. Cats, for example, have been associated with good and bad luck. Birds were thought of as messengers[2] and symbols of death, bad fortune, or peace. Many of the animals that have been written about

Reading fluently means getting the main idea of the reading without slowing down to look up words in your dictionary.

5

over the years, such as the dove, black cat, or bat, can still be found on earth today. There are some creatures, though, that many people believe cannot be found anywhere; the unicorn is one such animal.

10 The unicorn is perhaps the most mystical of all creatures talked and written about over the centuries. In ancient Greek and Roman myths, it was believed to represent purity, chastity,[3] and innocence. In Chinese mythology, the unicorn is an animal that symbolizes good fortune. Some believe that the reason unicorns have not been seen for many centuries is because we are living in 'bad' times, and that unicorns will 15 appear again when goodness exists on earth.

People have described the unicorn as a white animal that looks like a horse; some believe that it has the legs and hooves[4] of a deer. Its most recognizable and unique feature, however, is the single horn (or the uni-horn) that projects from the middle of its forehead. During the Middle 20 Ages,[5] people believed a unicorn's horn could cure many illnesses and neutralize[6] poison. As it was considered very valuable, a powdered form of 'Unicorn's Horn' was sold in many druggist's shops.

Did unicorns ever really exist? This is a question that remains unanswered today. Some believe that, like the dragon, the unicorn never 25 existed and was simply an animal from a fairy tale or mythology. Others believe that the unicorn still exists in remote regions of the earth, and can be seen only by people of exceptional[7] virtue and honesty. There are still others who believe that the unicorn was a type of sacred animal that came to earth from heaven and eventually became 30 a human in order to survive. Someday, they believe, these humans will become unicorns once again. A final point of view is that, like the dinosaur, unicorns once existed but became extinct. This theory suggests that because the unicorn's horn was used as a type of medicine, humans hunted the animal out of existence.

35 Animals such as the narwhal may provide evidence, or give us a clue, that unicorns once existed on earth. The male narwhal is a huge sea creature that can be found in the Arctic seas. This animal has a single horn, or tusk, that projects from its forehead—similar to that of the unicorn. In fact, in the seventeenth century, people often confused the 40 narwhal's tusk with the horn of the unicorn. The similarity of the male narwhal to the unicorn has led some people to believe that perhaps the unicorn is the narwhal's ancestor, or vice versa. Although narwhals have also been hunted for centuries, they may have escaped extinction for different reasons: they are only found in certain parts of the world, 45 and are hunted by only a relatively small number of people.

Although there is no evidence that the unicorn exists in the present day, it is still written and talked about in books, on websites and on television. In the popular American TV show *Ally McBeal*, for example, a unicorn appeared to people who were considered honest and virtuous. Whichever theory you choose to believe about the unicorn, one thing is certain, people throughout history seem to have been captured by its beauty, magic, and mystery.

50

---

¹ **superstition** a belief related to magic or luck, not based on reason or fact
² **messenger** a person or animal that delivers a message such as a letter or note
³ **chastity** the state of being sexually pure, of never having sexual relations
⁴ **hoof** the pointed, hard foot of certain animals, such as horses, pigs, deer
⁵ **the Middle Ages** the period in European history from approximately 500 A.D. to 1500 A.D.
⁶ **neutralize** to reduce or destroy the power of something that is normally dangerous or harmful
⁷ **exceptional** very special, extraordinary

Reading Comprehension: How Much Do You Remember?

Ⓐ How much do you remember from the reading? Choose the best answer for each of the questions or statements below.

1. The reading says that _____ have been symbols of both good and bad luck.
   a. unicorns   **b.** cats   **c.** bats

2. The word *unicorn* refers to the animal's _____.
   a. hoofed feet   **b.** color   **c.** one horn

3. Ancient Greek and Roman myths often described the unicorn as _____.
   a. lucky and powerful   **b.** pretty and friendly   **c.** pure and innocent

4. During the Middle Ages, people believed the unicorn's horn could be used as a kind of _____.
   a. medicine   **b.** poison   **c.** make-up

5. Which of the following is NOT a belief about unicorns mentioned in the reading?
   a. Unicorns were hunted by humans and became extinct.
   b. Some humans became unicorns in order to survive.
   c. Today, only very honest people can see unicorns.

6. According to the reading, some people believe that _____ is related to the unicorn.
   a. a female horse   **b.** a male sea creature   **c.** neither a nor b

7. The narwhal _____.
   a. exists only in fairy tales   **b.** is now extinct
   c. lives in a very cold habitat

Ⓑ Check your answers with a partner. Count how many you get correct—be honest! Then, fill in the Reading Comprehension Chart on page 202.

Vocabulary Comprehension: Word Definitions

Ⓐ Match each vocabulary item on the left with a definition on the right.

1. myth _____
2. mystical _____
3. remote _____
4. project _____
5. sacred _____
6. evidence _____
7. ancestor _____
8. virtue _____
9. fairy tale _____

a. proof or fact that shows that something is true or possible

b. a good quality or characteristic; a kind of goodness in a person

c. related to God, holy

d. a person or thing that came first or earlier, that others are related to

e. a children's story that usually includes magical events and creatures

f. magical, or mysterious in some way

g. an ancient, usually magical story used to explain an historical event

h. to stick out or extend from the surface or edge of something

i. distant, not close

Ⓑ Complete the sentences below using the vocabulary from A. Be sure to use the correct form of the word.

1. In some places in the world, the cow is considered a _____ animal.

2. Pedro is Mexican, but many of his _____ migrated from Spain three hundred years ago.

3. The Minotaur, a creature from ancient Greek mythology, is half bull, half man, with two sharp horns that _____ from its head.

4. If you're going to visit Alex's cabin, you should leave soon. He lives in a _____ part of the mountain that isn't easy to find.

5. Do you have any _____ that Simon robbed the bank, or do you just think he did it?

6. Almost every culture has its own creation _____, which explains how the world was made and how people were created.

7. My favorite _____ of all time is the story by the Brothers Grimm, *Hansel and Gretel*.

8. Which of the following words is a _____? Circle the correct answer: jealousy, love, pride.

9. In the movie, the hero has _____ powers that allow him to see into the future.

A What do you think the following words mean? Use the words to complete the sentences below.

(unique)   (biweekly)   (tricycle)
   (uniform)   (bilingual)   (triplets)

> In this chapter, you learned that the prefix 'uni-' means 'one,' or 'single,' as in the word 'unicorn.' Two other common prefixes used to show numbers in English are 'bi-,' meaning 'two' or 'twice,' and 'tri-' meaning 'three' or 'three times.'

1. Angela gave birth this morning, and she had _____! Two boys and a girl.

2. Many high school students are required to wear a school _____.

3. Tomoko is _____ in English and Japanese. She speaks and writes both languages fluently.

4. James bought his three-year-old niece a red _____ for her birthday. It won't be long before she's riding a real bike!

5. Can two people have the same fingerprints, or is it true that each person's fingerprints are _____?

6. I have a _____ magazine subscription. I get new issues in the mail on the first and fifteenth of each month.

B Now use *uni-*, *bi-*, or *tri-* to complete the sentences below. Check your answers with a partner.

1. I know that *The Godfather* is a _____logy, but I only saw the first of the three movies.

2. Look at that man over there riding a _____cycle. How can he keep his balance on a single wheel?

3. The Turkish-American Association is a _____national center in Turkey that helps to promote better understanding between the U.S. and Turkey.

4. A _____angle has three straight lines and three angles.

5. Can I use your _____noculars for a minute? The stage is so far away that I can't see anything.

6. The _____verse is made up of all the planets, stars, and galaxies that exist in space.

What Do You Think?

Discuss the following questions with a partner.

1. *Do you believe that the unicorn is only a mythical creature, or might it be the ancestor of the narwhal? Explain your answer.*

2. *Is there an animal, real or imaginary, that is common in myths in your country? Is this animal considered good or bad?*

3. *Are there any animals in your country that are considered sacred or holy?*

4. *Fairy tales often tell stories of good versus evil, or right versus wrong. Think of a fairy tale that you know well, and tell the story to your partner. Explain the message of the fairy tale.*

Real Life Skill

Dictionary Usage: Choosing the Right Word

In English, there are many words or phrases that are similar in meaning but are not exactly the same. In a good English-English dictionary, there will often be usage notes that compare the word or phrase with another, or explain how the word or phrase is used. Using these notes can help you choose the correct word or phrase.

(A) Read the dictionary entries below. Then, explain to a partner how the words *dead* and *extinct*, *exotic* and *foreign* are similar and different.

> ex·tinct *adj.* **1** something that is no longer in existence, specifically a type of animal, or plant, or an idea   *Dinosaurs became extinct about sixty million years ago.*
>
> dead *adj.* **1** no longer living, lifeless   *I think the woman has been dead for about two hours.*
>
> ex·ot·ic *adj.* **1** different, strange, foreign, usually in an interesting or exciting way   *Carmen prepared an exotic dish from southern Spain that was delicious.*
>
> for·eign *adj.* **1** located outside one's native country or area; non-native, different   *Hiroko speaks Japanese and two foreign languages.*

(B) Complete the sentences below with one of the words from A.

1. I've traveled all over my own country and, in addition, have visited five _____ countries.

2. There were once many dodo birds on the island of Mauritius in the Indian Ocean. Since the late 1800s, though, the bird has been _____.

3. I thought that Cary Grant, the actor, was still alive, but someone told me he's been _____ for more than ten years.

4. Many people think the white tiger is a(n) _____ and beautiful animal.

(C) Think of a synonym for a new word or phrase you learned in this unit. Can the word or phrase and its synonym be used in exactly the same way? Use your dictionary to help you.

Cultural Differences

Getting Ready

Discuss the following questions with a partner.

1. *Name one action that is considered good manners in your country. Name one that is considered bad manners.*

2. *What is happening in the pictures above? Tell your partner.*

3. *Are any of these actions, or gestures, considered offensive in your culture?*

4. *Do you know of any other cultural taboos?*

Before You Read:
Acceptable Behavior

Ⓐ Look at the chart. Are these types of behavior acceptable in your country? Check (✔) Acceptable or Unacceptable.

Type of behavior	Acceptable	Unacceptable
1. raising your voice in a public place		
2. looking someone in the eyes while speaking		
3. discussing religion with people you don't know well		
4. asking someone's age		
5. moving your hands while talking		
6. asking about someone's home life		

Ⓑ The following words are all in the reading passage:

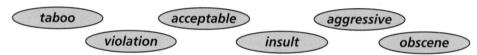

taboo   acceptable   aggressive   violation   insult   obscene

Look at the title of the reading. How do you think each word relates to the topic of the reading?

Reading Skill:
Identifying Main Ideas within Paragraphs

> *Every paragraph has a main idea, or topic, which gives us the most important information in that paragraph. Often the main idea is talked about in the first or second sentence of the paragraph.*

Ⓐ Skim the reading quickly and underline the main idea of each paragraph. Then, match each sentence below with the paragraph it describes. Write the number of the paragraph next to each sentence.

_____ Actions made with the hands have different meanings around the world.

_____ All cultures have types of behavior that are considered good or bad manners.

_____ In some cultures, there are topics that are not okay to discuss publicly. The volume of one's voice can also be taboo.

_____ Nonverbal taboos relate to messages we send with our bodies.

_____ Taboos are not the same everywhere; they are usually culture-specific.

_____ Remember that something that is okay in one culture may not be okay in another.

_____ Some body language using the hands or feet can offend others.

Ⓑ Compare your answers with a partner. Review the main ideas to get a summary of the reading.

Travel Manners

Every culture has its own unwritten list of behavior that is acceptable. Every society also has its taboos, or types of behavior that are considered a violation of good manners.[1] If you travel to another country, on business or vacation, it is helpful to learn some of that country's customs so that you don't insult the local people.

The word *taboo* comes from the Tongan[2] language and is used in modern English to describe verbal[3] and nonverbal behavior that is forbidden or to be avoided. In spite of what some may think, taboos are not universal;[4] they tend to be specific to a culture or country, and usually form around a group's values and beliefs. Therefore, what is considered acceptable behavior in one country may be a serious taboo in another.

Verbal taboos usually involve topics that people believe are too private to talk about publicly, or relate to one's manner of speaking. In many cultures, for example, it is considered bad manners and is often offensive to discuss subjects such as sex or religion in public. In some countries, the volume of one's voice may offend people. In Japan, for example, people tend to be more soft-spoken, and might think that someone who is speaking or laughing loudly is rude or aggressive.

Nonverbal taboos usually relate to body language. For example, one of the biggest differences among many Western, Asian, and African cultures is the use of eye contact. In the U.S., people make eye contact[5] when they talk to others. If a person avoids eye contact, others might think they are being dishonest or that they lack confidence.[6] If two people are having a conversation and the listener is not making eye contact, the speaker may think that the listener is not interested. In many Asian cultures, however, making direct eye contact with someone is often considered bold or aggressive. In many African cultures, making direct eye contact with an older person or a person of higher social rank or status is considered rude and disrespectful. In many Asian and African cultures, children are taught to lower their eyes when talking to their elders, or those of higher rank, as a way to show respect.

Certain actions, especially with the hands and feet, can cause offense in many cultures. In Thailand, as in most other Buddhist cultures in Asia, touching a person on the head is considered very insulting because the head is the highest, and therefore considered the most important, part of the body. As the feet are the lowest, pointing at someone with one of your feet, or showing the soles of your feet to someone, is considered insulting in many Asian countries.

Certain gestures[7] made with the hands can have very different meanings
40 depending on the country you are in. Crossing your middle finger over your
forefinger[8] is the sign for good luck in many western countries; in Vietnam
and Argentina, however, it is an obscene gesture. Making a V sign with the
forefinger and middle finger, with the palm of your hand turned toward
your body, is often used to mean a quantity of two. However, in the U.K.
45 and Australia, this gesture is obscene. Also, in some Asian countries, moving
your hands a lot while talking, or 'talking with your hands,' is considered
unseemly.

Behavior that is acceptable and non-offensive in one culture can be highly
offensive in another. When visiting a foreign country, be aware of some of
50 the basic differences, as this will help to ensure a more enjoyable trip.

---

1 **manners** set of behavior that is considered polite, suitable, acceptable
2 **Tonga** country in the southern Pacific Ocean
3 **verbal** spoken
4 **universal** existing everywhere, and being the same or similar for everyone
5 **make eye contact** to look a person in the eyes while talking with him or her
6 **confidence** belief in oneself; self-assuredness
7 **gesture** the movement of one's body, usually the head or hands, to express an idea
8 **forefinger** the finger next to the thumb, also called the index finger

---

(B)   Read the passage again, then answer the questions that follow.

Reading Comprehension:
What Do You Remember?

How much do you remember from the reading? Complete each sentence with the correct answer, then discuss your answers with a partner.

1. Before traveling to another country, it's often a good idea to _____
_____.

2. The word *taboo* means _____ and comes from the _____ language.

3. A taboo behavior is usually based on a group's _____.

4. In certain cultures, it is bad manners to discuss these topics in public:_____
_____.

5. In the U.S., people expect others to _____ when talking.
   In Asian and African cultures, people often avoid it because _____.

6. In many Asian cultures, it is very rude to touch a person on the _____,
   or to point at the person with your _____.

7. _____ is a sign of good luck in many Western countries,
   but it is _____ in Argentina and Vietnam.

Vocabulary Comprehension: Word Definitions

Ⓐ Look at the vocabulary items from the reading in the chart below. Write *noun*, *verb*, or *adjective* to describe each word's part of speech.

Ⓑ For each word or phrase, write the letter of the definition in the chart.

Vocabulary	Part of Speech	Definition
1. bold	adjective	g
2. violation		
3. insult		
4. forbidden		
5. value		
6. aggressive		
7. offensive		
8. unseemly		
9. obscene		

a. inappropriate, not suitable or proper

b. not allowed, to be avoided

c. to be rude to another with words or actions; to offend

d. extremely rude in a shocking way

e. very forceful or threatening with words or behavior

f. the breaking of a rule or law

g. daring, forward, willing to take risks

h. rude, unpleasant, insulting

i. a principle or quality considered worthwhile or desirable

Ⓒ Read each statement and circle the best answer. Then give one more example for each vocabulary item.

1. In many cultures, (spitting / talking) might be considered *offensive*.

2. (Stealing / Shopping) is *forbidden* almost everywhere.

3. In many countries, it might be *unseemly* for a man to wear (pants / shorts) to work.

4. A (sleeping cat / hungry dog) might be *aggressive*.

5. In many countries, students are considered to be *bold* if they disagree with their (teachers / classmates).

6. (Respect / Housing) for the elderly is an important *value* in many societies.

7. You might *insult* an American if you ask (his or her age / where he or she is from).

8. (Shaking hands / Raising the middle finger) is considered an *obscene* gesture in many countries.

9. It is a *violation* of good manners in many Asian countries to enter a home with your shoes (on / off).

Vocabulary Skill:
Creating Word Webs

One helpful strategy that you can use to memorize new vocabulary is to create a word web. Word webs can help you remember the meaning of new vocabulary and relate this vocabulary to other words you know.

There are many ways to organize a word web. Look at the example below. Think about the new vocabulary you learned in this chapter. Many of the words relate to the topic of *behavior*.

Ⓐ Complete the diagram below using the words in the box. Then, add other words or phrases you learned in this chapter. Explain your diagram to a partner.

| verbal | nonverbal | obscene | offensive | make eye contact |

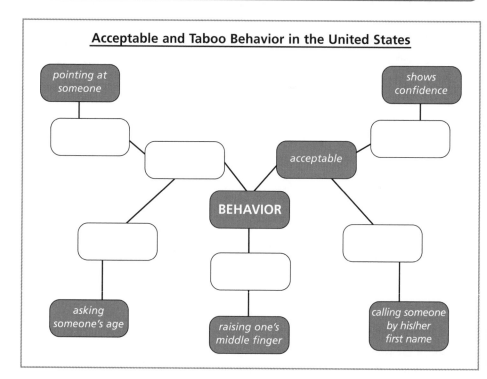

Acceptable and Taboo Behavior in the United States

Ⓑ Using vocabulary you've learned in this chapter, create a new word web that describes acceptable and taboo behavior in your country.

Think About It   Discuss the following questions with a partner.

1. *Imagine someone is going to visit your country. Make a list of three acceptable and three taboo forms of behavior this visitor should know about.*

2. *In your country, are there any forms of behavior that used to be considered unseemly or offensive, that aren't anymore?*

3. *Do you think people's values in your country have changed much in recent years?*

4. *Have you, or has someone you know, ever done something that offended a person from another country?*

Discuss the following questions with a partner.

1. What are some things you can do to learn about another country's customs?
2. Have you, or has anyone you know, ever visited a foreign country?
3. Can you think of some general rules a person should follow when visiting any foreign country?
4. The following words can all be found in the reading:

adapt   conservative   tolerant   precaution   sensitive   critical

Look at the title of the reading. How is each word related to the topic of the reading?

Reading Skill:
Developing
Reading
Fluency

Time yourself as you read through the passage. Try to read as fluently as you can. Record your time in the Reading Rate Chart on page 202.

Avoiding Cultural Taboos _____

The speed and convenience[1] of modern travel means that destinations that used to take a long time to travel to can now be reached quickly and easily. Even though 'faraway' countries may now seem closer thanks to air travel, they may still be different from your home country. Therefore, it is important to adapt your behavior so that you don't insult or offend the local people. Following are some fundamental rules that will make communication easier, and your trip more enjoyable.

> Improve your reading fluency by not stopping at every word you don't know. Focus on understanding the 'gist,' or general idea, of what you are reading.

First, never raise your voice in order to make yourself understood. If you do not know the word for something in the local language, or cannot make yourself understood verbally, try drawing a picture, or pointing to an object. Remember, though, that pointing directly at a person can be highly offensive in some cultures. If you have to point something out, do so by gesturing towards the object, with the palm of your hand flat, facing upward, and your fingers outstretched.[2] Before you travel, try learning some basic words or phrases of the local language. Most useful are those that express gratitude and politeness such as words for *please, thank you,* and *may I,* as well as basic greetings.

Second, consider the main religion of the country you plan to visit and read about any taboos related to clothing, especially if you plan to visit places that are considered sacred. As a precaution, bring conservative clothes, such as shirts or T-shirts that cover your shoulders, and long trousers.

Avoid topics of conversation that you think may be sensitive. If a topic is sensitive in your own culture, it will more than likely be the same in other cultures. Feel free to show interest in the history and customs of the place you are visiting, but don't ask too many questions about why things are done a certain way; you may offend the local people.

Keep in mind that in many cultures, displaying[3] affection in public is considered taboo. Kissing on the street or in public places is unacceptable behavior and should be avoided. If you are unsure of how to behave, watch the local people and copy them—if they don't behave in a certain way, you probably shouldn't either.

Finally, if you are traveling on business, or plan to stay with a host family, and you wish to take a gift, do some research. The idea of the perfect gift varies greatly from country to country, and one of the easiest ways to offend somebody is to give the wrong gift. In China, it is taboo to give clocks and fans. The Chinese word for 'fan' has a similar sound to the word for 'separation,' while the sound for 'clock' is similar to that of 'death.' In Japan, gifts should never be given in sets of 'four,' as the sound of the word 'four' in Japanese is similar to the sound of the word meaning 'death.'

The opening of gifts is also treated very differently around the world. In many Western countries, do not be surprised if your hosts immediately tear the wrapping paper from a gift in great excitement. They will then tell you how wonderful the gift is, even if they do not like it! In most Asian countries, it is considered impolite to open gifts in front of the gift-giver for fear of offending the person.

50

Wherever you go in the world, always be tolerant of the local customs. Avoid being critical; try instead to show respect for the values of the country you are in, even if you do not necessarily agree with them.

55

---

¹ **convenience** something that makes life easier
² **outstretched** stretched or extended out
³ **displaying** showing; expressing emotion through gestures

---

Reading Comprehension: How Much Do You Remember?

A For each question or statement, choose the best answer.

1. The reading lists _____ main things that travelers can do to avoid insulting locals while visiting another country.
   a. three   **b.** four   **c.** five

2. While in another country, if a local can't understand something you are saying, try _____.
   a. saying it louder   **b.** drawing or pointing   **c.** learning some basic words

3. According to the reading, which articles of clothing should you plan to travel with?
   a. a T-shirt and shorts   **b.** a jacket and hat   **c.** pants and a long-sleeve shirt

4. If a topic isn't appropriate to talk about in your country, it probably _____ okay to talk about in another country.
   a. might be   **b.** should be   **c.** isn't

5. According to the reading, _____ is not appropriate behavior in many countries.
   a. kissing in public   **b.** expressing gratitude   **c.** giving presents

6. According to the reading, the best gift to give someone from China is _____.
   a. a fan   **b.** a clock   **c.** neither a nor b

7. Which is true? Americans will usually _____.
   a. not open a gift immediately
   b. open a gift in front of the gift-giver
   c. say nothing about the gift

B Check your answers with a partner. Count how many you got correct—be honest! Then, fill in the Reading Comprehension Chart on page 202.

Vocabulary Comprehension: Odd Word Out

(A) For each group, circle the word that does not belong. The words in *italics* are vocabulary items from the reading.

1. maintain   change   *adapt*   alter
2. *precaution*   carelessness   safety   protection
3. traditional   *conservative* old-fashioned modern
4. accepting   *critical*   *tolerant*   understanding
5. *gratitude*   thanks   disapproval   appreciation
6. *fundamental*   important   main   unnecessary
7. love   fondness   *affection*   dislike
8. public   *sensitive*   private   personal

(B) Complete the sentences using the words in *italics* from A. Be sure to use the correct form of the word.

1. When Jamie moved into her own apartment, it took her a while to _____ to living alone.

2. Clara's father has some very _____ beliefs. For example, he thinks a woman shouldn't work after she gets married.

3. After receiving a gift in the U.S., it's common to send a thank-you card to express one's _____.

4. The president thinks this information is too _____ to share with the public right now.

5. Jack's parents are too _____ of their son's bad behavior. They let him do whatever he likes.

6. Hiromi has a great deal of _____ for her grandfather, and visits him at least once a week.

7. As a _____, make sure the windows and doors of your house are locked before you travel.

8. Kristin and Marcus may disagree a lot, but they try never to be _____ of each other's opinions.

9. What do you think are the _____ differences between cultures of the East and the West?

Vocabulary Skill:

Organizing Vocabulary

One helpful way to remember new words is to group them into meaningful categories, for example, by part of speech or topic. Organizing your vocabulary can also help you to relate new vocabulary to other words you know.

A One way to organize words is to group them by part of speech. Write the part of speech for each word below.

conservative _____	critical _____	tolerant _____
fundamental _____	local _____	sensitive _____
acceptable _____	insulting _____	forbidden _____
offensive _____	aggressive _____	obscene _____
unseemly _____	precaution _____	confident _____

B Another way to organize these words is to use a more descriptive category —for example, words that are *positive*, *negative*, or *neutral*. Put the adjectives from A into one or all of the categories below.

Positive Meaning	Negative Meaning	Neutral
tolerant	critical	local

C Vocabulary can also be grouped by topic. What are some topics that you can use to organize the adjectives above? Think of a topic, and then list the adjectives from A that relate to it in the chart below. Share your ideas with a partner.

Topic	Adjectives

What Do You Think?

Discuss the following questions with a partner.

1. *Imagine that you and your partner are planning a trip to a country whose culture is very different from yours. List some of the ways you would need to adapt your behavior while visiting.*

2. *Do people often give gifts in your country? For what reasons? Imagine a friend is coming to visit your family. What would be an appropriate gift to give your parents?*

3. *Do you think people in your country are tolerant of different beliefs and lifestyles? Explain your answer.*

4. *Do you think there are fundamental differences between your country and countries such as the U.S. or the U.K.? What are some of the similarities?*

Real Life Skill

Expressing Yourself Online

When we communicate with others face to face, we can understand their meaning from their words, and from behavior such as nonverbal cues (e.g., smiling) and verbal cues (e.g. a raised voice). Due to the lack of visual and verbal cues in online communications—especially e-mail—people sometimes use symbols, abbreviations, and capital letters for emphasis or to express certain feelings. Learning some of these common forms can help you to understand a writer's meaning better.

(A) Look at some of the common ways to express feelings and opinions in writing online. Are any of these rules different in your country?

Method of expression	Example	Used to...
Emoticons (also called *smileys*)	:-) happy :-(unhappy ;-) winking; laughing or teasing	show feelings or emotions
Abbreviations	LOL = Laughing out loud OIC = Oh, I see! CU = See you! BTW = By the way	show feelings, or say something faster
ALL CAPS	PLEASE CALL ME Tom ISN'T home.	shout or say something loudly, or emphasize something
Asterisks * *	I had a *great* time.	emphasize something

* Note: Capitalizing all the letters in a word or sentence is often considered rude.

(B) Look at the sentences below. How are they different? Say each aloud to your partner.

Mark called. :-)   Mark called. :-(MARK CALLED.   *Mark* called.

(C) Read the e-mail below. How does Amy feel? Explain her e-mail to a partner.

Dear Soo Hyun,
Just a quick e-mail to let you know that I'm not arriving in Korea until June 30. :-(The travel agent here in the U.S. booked my ticket for that date instead of the 26th. Can you come to meet me at the airport on the 30th? PLEASE E-MAIL ME, and let me know. I'm *really* looking forward to meeting you again.
CU soon :-)
Amy
BTW - my brother says 'Hi!'

Money

Getting Ready

Discuss the following questions with a partner.

1. *Finish this sentence: If I won a million dollars, I would _____.*
   Explain your answer.
2. *Who is the richest person in your country? Would you like to be this person? Why or why not?*
3. *Is there a lottery in your country? How much money can you win?*
4. *Do you think having a lot of money can guarantee happiness? Why or why not?*

Before You Read:

Money
Knowledge

(A) Look at the list of sentences in the chart. Match each cause with an effect.

Cause (reason)

1. This area has become very popular among homebuyers in recent years.
2. Many game shows now offer over a million dollars in prize money.
3. Danny spent all his lottery winnings within a few weeks.
4. Yong-jin won the top prize on last week's *Win a Million!* show.
5. The cost of education has increased in recent years.

Effect (result)

_____ **a.** Housing is now very expensive here.

_____ **b.** He's taking his family on a round-the-world vacation.

_____ **c.** Many students have to work part-time to pay for their schooling.

_____ **d.** The popularity of game shows has increased in recent years.

_____ **e.** Now he doesn't have any of the money left.

(B) Look at the examples of how cause and effect can be joined.

> *Examples:*
> - *Housing is now very expensive here **because** this area has become very popular among homebuyers in recent years.*
> - *This area has become very popular among homebuyers in recent years. **As a result**, housing is very expensive here.*

With a partner, make similar sentences using the information in the chart. Use the words *because* and *due to (the fact that)* to talk about cause; use the words *as a result*, *so*, and *therefore* to talk about effect.

(C) The following words are all in the reading passage:

cost of living   demand   property   inflation   retirement   expenses

How do you think these words relate to the topic of money?

Ⓐ Skim the passage below and complete the chart with information from the reading. Then, compare your answers with a partner.

Cause (reason)	Effect (result)
1. There are more people living in an area, but fewer homes for sale or rent.	Housing has become very expensive.
2.	Living in a city center is more expensive than ever.
3. Prices have gone up, but the value of money has gone down.	
4. Many retired people now rent their housing.	
5. Many older people are living longer lives.	
6.	A million dollars may not be enough to live on.

What Does a Million Dollars Buy? _____

People often think that having a million dollars would make all their dreams come true. There are TV game shows that give contestants[1] the chance to become millionaires. Many people on these shows probably believe that with this money, they could do anything or go anywhere. In reality, 'a million' may not really be that much money. When asked the question "What would you do with a million dollars?" most people tend to give similar answers: "Quit my job," "Buy my dream house," or "Go traveling." Twenty years ago, it was possible to realize these dreams. However, things are not so easy today. 5

In many developed countries,[2] the cost of living is higher than ever. One of 10 the main reasons for this is demand. Over the last twenty years, for example, housing prices in many of the world's cities have soared. The main reason is that there are more people living in certain areas, but there is less housing available there for sale or rent. For example, in the U.S., luxury[3] homes in the state of Arizona sold for about $800,000 in 1995. These same 15 homes now cost more than $1.5 million. Now, because more people live in the area, the cost of property has risen.

Apartments in many city centers are also more expensive now than in the

past. In the recent past, people often moved from a city center to other city
neighborhoods or the suburbs[4] in order to escape overcrowding and noise.
Today, people want to be closer to their workplace, and many are now
moving back into the city center. As a result, living in or near this area costs
more than ever. Apartments in London's Mayfair district or in Manhattan in
New York City often sell for over a million dollars. Many of these modern
apartment complexes have indoor swimming pools or movie theaters that
allow people to relax or exercise without leaving their building.

Inflation is another important reason for the rise in the cost of living. Over
the last 150 years, as prices have gone up, the value of money has gone
down, so we now need more money to buy things. In 1850, for example,
$50,000 had as much buying power as $1 million dollars does today. Of
course, people now earn more money than they did 150 years ago, but they
also spend more on necessities such as food, medicine, and housing.

In order to live well after you stop working, you should begin saving for
retirement early. Experts suggest that after you retire, you will need 75
percent to 80 percent of your salary to live on every month. In other words,
if you make $3,000 per month while working, you will need between
$2,250 and $2,400 per month to live on during retirement. This calculation[5]
assumes that you have no mortgage[6] on a house to continue paying, or any
other major expenses. However, many retired people now rent their housing,
and so they will pay more money in housing costs over time. Older people
now also have to spend more on health care because they live longer; many
people in developed countries now live into their eighties or nineties.

Due to increased demand for housing, higher inflation, and longer life
expectancy,[7] a million may not be enough to live on. Of course, where you
live and how long you live will influence how much a million dollars can
buy. To be able to retire early, travel the world, and build your dream home,
you may have to appear on that game show and win more than once!

---

1 **contestant** a person who plays a game to try and win money or other prizes
2 **developed country** a country that has a high standard of living and is usually strong economically
3 **luxury** beautiful, expensive, very comfortable
4 **suburb** a mainly residential town or area outside of a large city
5 **calculation** the act of doing math or making a guess about something, usually using numbers
6 **mortgage** a bank loan for a house or piece of land, usually paid back over a period of years
7 **life expectancy** how long a person or group of people are expected to live

Ⓑ   Now read the passage again, then answer the questions that follow.

How much do you remember from the reading? Complete the sentences with the correct answer, then discuss your answers with a partner.

1. In 2000, a luxury home in Arizona cost _____; in 1995, it cost _____.

2. In the past, people moved out of the city center because _____
_____.

3. In 1850, $_____ was worth about $_____ in today's money.

4. People generally make more money today; however, _____.

5. Experts suggest that a person should _____ early in life.

6. If you make $4,000 per month, you will need _____ per month after you retire.

7. The calculation in question 6 assumes two things. What are they?
_____

A Look at the list of words from the reading. Match each word or phrase with a definition on the right.

1. realize   _____
2. cost of living   _____
3. soar   _____
4. demand   _____
5. property   _____
6. inflation   _____
7. retirement   _____
8. assume   _____
9. expenses   _____

a. to go very high, usually by flying
b. to believe that something is true without knowing for sure
c. things that one owns; often used to talk about one's house or land
d. the period of time after one stops working
e. things that one must pay for regularly, e.g., rent, food, bills
f. to make something happen or to make it real; to fulfill
g. a great need for something
h. the amount of money required for life's necessities, e.g., food, housing, etc.
i. a continuing increase in prices over time

B Complete the sentences below using the words from A. Be sure to use the correct form of the word.

1. There is a high _____ for nurses in the United States right now.

2. You can't live on $800 a month in New York! The _____ is too high.

3. After saving for years, Yumi bought a _____ in Tokyo.

4. Some people in the U.S. choose early _____ and stop working at 59.

5. Temperatures this weekend are expected to _____ to record highs.

6. To _____ your dream of becoming a doctor, you must finish university.

7. After Sylvia pays her monthly _____, she is left with only $100.

8. _____ caused gas and food prices to rise by 2 percent this year.

9. Don't _____ you'll have enough money when you retire, save now.

Vocabulary Skill:
The Prefix *in-*

In this chapter, you read the word 'inflation.' This word begins with the prefix 'in-,' meaning 'in' or 'into.' The prefix 'in-' can also mean 'not.' When the prefix 'in-' comes before the letter l, the prefix changes to 'il-;' before m or p, it changes to 'im-;' before r, it changes to 'ir-.'

Ⓐ **What do you think the following words mean? Complete the sentences below with the words.**

install	illustration	inseparable	import
illogical	immature	irresponsible	

1. Use an _____ to explain new words. This will make it easier for beginning students to understand.

2. It was _____ of you to stay out late the night before final exams. What were you thinking?

3. Marco may be 30 years old, but he's very _____. He behaves like he's 16!

4. Young-ju works for a Canadian company that plans to _____ ginseng from Korea and China.

5. Before you can use the computer, you need to _____ new software.

6. I thought Cathy's explanation was completely _____. It didn't make any sense to me.

7. Atsushi and his brother are _____. They go everywhere together.

Ⓑ **Now use *in-*, *il-*, *im-*, or *ir-* to complete the words below. Then, explain the meaning of each word to a partner.**

1. There are still people in the U.S. that are functionally ____literate—meaning they can hardly read or write.

2. The doctors saved Emilo's life by removing his heart and ____planting an artificial one instead.

3. Here's the list of ____gredients you'll need to make the soup: salt, water, chicken, flour, and onions.

4. Sandra has an ____rational fear of spiders. She's much bigger than they are, after all.

5. During December, the city center was ____luminated by hundreds of colored lights.

6. The government is trying to ____rigate the desert by bringing in water from a river miles away.

7. Cancer is still an ____curable disease.

8. After waiting for Maria for twenty minutes, Albert began to get ____patient.

Think About It | **Discuss the following questions with a partner.**

1. *Can you name any millionaires or billionaires in the world? What about in your country? What do they do?*

2. *What could you buy with one million units of the currency in your country?*

3. *What is the most expensive city in your country? Why does it cost a lot to live there?*

Discuss the following questions with a partner.

1. Do you know anyone who has won a lottery or received a lot of money all at one time? What did he or she do with the money?

2. What should a person do right after winning or receiving a lot of money?

3. What bad things can happen to people who win a lottery?

4. The following words are all in the reading:

purchase   fortune   broke
invest   affluent   run out

What does each word mean? How does each word relate to the topic of the reading?

Time yourself as you read through the passage. Try to read as fluently as you can. Record your time in the Reading Rate Chart on page 202.

Reading Skill:

Developing
Reading
Fluency

Lottery Winners—Rich, but Happy? _____

Every week, millions of dollars are spent, and won, on lottery tickets. The jackpot[1] in many lotteries can be as much as 100 million, and winners suddenly find themselves with more money than ever before. Many will have enough to purchase a new car, build a luxury house, take a holiday, and quit working—all within a short amount of time. The lucky few who hit the jackpot,[2] however, may end up with problems—more than they had before they struck it rich.[3]

Remember to use the skills you have learned to help you read fluently; predicting, scanning, and skimming can all help you read more fluently.

5

Lottery organizers employ counselors to help jackpot winners. These counselors encourage winners to get advice from financial experts such
10 as accountants,[4] about how best to invest their windfall. The counselors also help winners to understand how their lives may change for the better—and possibly for the worse. Luckily, many jackpot winners manage their fortunes sensibly.[5] Some winners, however, do not use their money wisely and, as a result, end up in debt[6] and struggling to
15 make ends meet.

The biggest mistake many lottery winners make is overspending. A waiter who won $2 million in a California lottery spent all of his winnings shopping, having parties, and lending money to friends. A few months after he won, he was broke and working as a sales clerk.

20 Being greedy[7] is another way to invite trouble. In 1999, a woman from California was ordered to pay her ex-husband her entire lottery winnings. She won a $1.3 million lottery jackpot eleven days before her divorce from her husband was finalized. Under the state law, her spouse was entitled to half the winnings. However, the woman didn't tell her
25 husband about the win, and used her mother's address to receive the money. Two years later, the divorced man received a letter for his wife from a lottery winners advisory company. It was then that he discovered his ex-wife's secret win.

Another problem that many lottery winners often experience is
30 unwanted attention from the public or their colleagues at work. Many winners have to deal with letters or e-mail from strangers asking for money. Other lottery winners who do not immediately quit their jobs may find that their less affluent colleagues expect them to pay for lunch all the time, or to loan them money.

35 Not all jackpot winners experience the same fate,[8] though. A woman from south Wales who won over £7 million in the U.K.'s National Lottery gave £3 million of her winnings to family and friends. The biggest luxury item she bought right after winning was a secondhand[9] Porsche.

40 No matter how large the jackpot, there is always a risk that the money will run out if a winner overspends and does not invest wisely. Lottery winners should remember that they often have to pay a large amount of their winnings to the government in taxes. Over time, inflation also reduces the value of a windfall.

45 Financial advisors agree that people who win a lottery should follow a

few simple rules to ensure the future of their fortune. First, meet with an accountant or other financial advisor. Second, pay all debts, such as home mortgages, car loans, and credit card bills. Finally, a winner should calculate how much money they will need to live on every year for the rest of his or her life. From that calculation, financial advisors say a person will know exactly how much money should be invested, and how much is left to spend. Only then, advisors suggest, should a lottery winner plan to hand in his or her resignation[10] to the boss.

50

---

1 **jackpot** the biggest or most expensive prize given in a contest
2 **hit the jackpot** to win the top prize in a contest
3 **strike it rich** to become rich suddenly
4 **accountant** a person who keeps financial records and gives financial advice to a person or company
5 **sensibly** logically, wisely, carefully
6 **in debt** owing money to others
7 **greedy** extremely selfish; keeping all of something for oneself
8 **fate** outcome or event, that one cannot usually control, e.g., death
9 **secondhand** used before
10 **resignation** a letter to an employer telling them one will quit a job

---

Reading Comprehension: How Much Do You Remember?

(A) Decide if the following statements about the reading are true (*T*) or false (*F*). If you check (✔) false, correct the statement to make it true.

	T	F
1. Some lottery winners' lives improve after they win, but some winners' lives get worse.		
2. Lottery organizers hire financial experts to help winners manage their money.		
3. A woman won over a million dollars and spent it all in a few months.		
4. According to California state law, a person's spouse has the right to take half of the person's lottery winnings.		
5. A Welsh woman won the lottery and immediately spent £3 million.		
6. According to the reading, taxes and inflation will eventually lower the original value of the lottery win.		
7. Financial advisors suggest that lottery winners do two things to avoid losing their fortune.		

(B) Check your answers with a partner. Count how many you got correct—be honest! Then fill in the Reading Comprehension Chart on page 202.

Vocabulary Comprehension:
Words in Context

Ⓐ The words in *italics* are vocabulary items from the reading. Read each question or statement and choose the correct answer. Compare your answers with a partner.

1. Which would you *purchase*?
   a. a computer   **b.** your health

2. A person who is *broke* might try to _____.
   a. spend some money   **b.** get a loan

3. In many countries in the world, which are people *entitled* to?
   a. medical care   **b.** a lottery ticket

4. A person with a *fortune* will probably _____.
   a. have to work all of his life **b.** be able to retire early

5. If you *run out* of something, you'll probably need to _____.
   a. study harder   **b.** get more

6. You have some money saved, and decide to *invest* this money in _____ in order to _____.
   a. property / make more money   **b.** presents / spend some money

7. A *windfall* is a large amount of money that someone _____.
   a. saves for patiently   **b.** receives suddenly

8. It might be hard to *make ends meet* if you _____.
   a. lose your job   **b.** get a pay raise

9. Which person would probably be considered *affluent*?
   a. an office worker   **b.** a millionaire

Ⓑ Now think of other examples using the vocabulary from A. Share your ideas with a partner.

1. What was the last thing you *purchased*?

2. Have you ever been *broke*?

3. Name something else that people in most countries are *entitled* to.

4. How might a person make a *fortune*?

5. Name something you might *run out* of.

6. How else could you *invest* your money?

7. Why might someone receive a *windfall* of money?

8. Why else might it be hard to *make ends meet*?

9. Can you think of a synonym for *affluent*?

Vocabulary Skill:
Noun and Adjective Suffixes -ent and -ant

Ⓐ Complete each definition below with the correct *-ent* or *-ant* word. Use your dictionary to help you with spelling. Is each word a noun, adjective, or both?

1. a person that lives or resides in a certain place   r **_esident_**

2. a person or thing that is pleasing to you   p _____

3. something or someone that is unlike another   d _____

4. something that is immediate, quick, very fast   i _____

5. a place that people go to eat a meal   r _____

6. empty, unoccupied   v _____

7. an unfortunate happening, a mishap; e.g., a car ____   a _____

8. a happening or occurrence   e _____

> *In this chapter, you learned the word 'affluent,' which ends with the suffix '-ent,' and 'accountant' which ends with the suffix '-ant.' These suffixes can both be used to describe someone or something that performs or causes a specific action, e.g., servant: someone that serves. The suffixes '-ent' and '-ant' are used with both nouns and adjectives.*

Ⓑ Think of two more words that end with *-ent* or *-ant*. Write a definition for each and see if your partner can guess the words.

Ⓒ Complete the reading below with the correct forms of the *-ent* or *-ant* words from A. You can use the same word more than once.

Some people become rich by winning the lottery or playing the stock market. Have you ever wondered what it would be like to become a(n) (1)_____ millionaire? Here are some true stories about how people made a lot of money quickly in the United States:

A seventy-nine-year-old New Mexico (2)_____ dropped a cup of coffee she bought from a fast-food (3)_____ on her lap, causing serious burns to her legs and lower body. She sued* the (4)_____ for a million dollars and won.

In 1997, a Delaware woman fell from the bathroom window of a popular nightclub. The woman was trying to climb through the window to avoid paying a $3.50 entrance charge. In the (5)_____, she broke her two front teeth. She sued the club for $12,000 and won.

In 1998, a Pennsylvania man was robbing a house. The house was (6)_____ because the owners were away on vacation. The man got locked in the garage and was unable to get out. For eight days, until the (7)_____ returned, the man lived on dog food and soda. He sued the homeowners for $500,000 for his suffering and won.

In 2000, a Texas woman was shopping in a furniture store. She fell over a child who was running around in the store, and broke her ankle. The woman sued the storeowners for $780,000 and won. Here's the strange thing about this (8)_____: the child she fell over was *her* son.

*sue: to take legal action against someone, usually to get compensation for an injustice
Source: http://www.dumblaws.com/ubb/ForumII/HTML/000069.html

What Do You Think?

Discuss the following questions with a partner.

1. *Do you ever buy lottery tickets? Have you ever won any money?*
2. *There is a saying, 'Money cannot buy happiness.' Do you agree or disagree? Explain your answer.*
3. *Which do you think is more important for a happy life—health or wealth? Why?*

Real Life Skill

Money and Banking

If you're planning a trip to an English-speaking country, especially if you plan to stay for an extended period of time, it is often helpful to learn about money and banking practices. Becoming familiar with some of the local banking customs as well as some of the common money and banking terms will help you to better enjoy your stay.

(A) The following are common words and phrases used in many English-speaking countries. Discuss their meanings with a partner.

Forms of Payment	Getting Money from a Machine	At the Bank
cash	ATM*	open a checking account
check	PIN**	currency exchange
debit card	withdraw	money transfer
check card	deposit	
credit card	balance	
	receipt	

*Automated Teller Machine   **Personal Indentification Number

(B) Complete the information below using words and phrases from the chart.

1. Below is a common form of payment in the U.S. What is it? Imagine you need to pay $55.35 to Kean's Department Store. Complete the missing information.

> 811
>
> 222 Shannon Street   Date: _____
> San Francisco, CA 94134
>
> Pay to _____
> The order of _____ $ [   ]
> _____
>
>   Bank of America   _____

2. In many countries, you might use a _____ to reserve a hotel room.

3. You want to send or receive money electronically. You should visit a bank or a credit agency and ask about _____.

4. You have money from your country, but you need American dollars. You should visit a place that does _____.

5. You have $500 in your checking account. You go to the ATM and _____ $85. What is your _____ now?

Fashion and Style

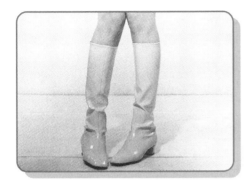

Getting Ready

Discuss the following questions with a partner.

1. *Look at the photos above. Describe what the people in each photo are wearing. Use the following vocabulary to help you:*

> miniskirt   platform shoes   high heels
>
> go-go boots   bow tie

2. *Describe the clothes you are wearing at the moment. What do your clothes tell people about you?*
3. *How do men's and women's fashions differ?*
4. *Do you consider yourself to be a fashion-conscious person? Explain your answer.*

Before You Read:
How Trendy Are You?

Discuss the following questions with a partner.

1. What do you understand by the word *fashionable*? Name a person who you think is fashionable.

2. What is the most fashionable article of clothing you own?

3. What fashions are 'in style' right now? How are today's fashions similar to or different from fashions of twenty years ago?

4. The following words and phrases can all be found in the reading. What does each mean? How does each word relate to the topic of the reading?

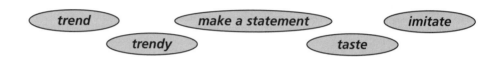

trend   make a statement   imitate

trendy   taste

Reading Skill:
Skimming for the Main Idea

Skimming is one way to look for the main ideas in a reading. When we skim we read over parts of the text very quickly. We don't need to read every word, or look up words we don't understand; we just need to get a general idea of what something is about.

Ⓐ Skim the passage quickly. Read only the *title*, the *first and last paragraphs*, and the *first sentence of the other paragraphs*. Don't worry about words you don't know. Then, complete the sentence.

This reading is mainly about _____.

1. clothing makers who have created some of the world's most important fashions

2. why fashion styles from the 1960s, '70s, and '80s are still popular today

3. what fashion is and which fashions have been most important in recent decades

Fashionable Decisions _____

One of the first decisions many people make in the morning is what to wear. Our clothes make a statement about our individual style and beliefs; they can also say something about our musical tastes, or our cultural identity. Fashion trends change not only with the
5 seasons but also annually, with new styles being introduced, as well as old ones revived, on the catwalks[1] of Paris, Milan, London, and New York. Looking back at changes in clothing styles over the past few decades, it seems that fashion trends tend to occur in cycles. What was fashionable twenty years ago, for example, may come
10 back into fashion again in the near future. You only have to pick up any fashion magazine to find lists of what is considered 'in' or 'out' of fashion at the moment.

Fashion trends are influenced by more than just a few well-known clothing designers. Celebrities such as movie stars, pop musicians,
15 and royalty also influence which fashions are 'trendy.' In the 1950s,

Elvis Presley's style was copied by millions around the world. White T-shirts, patent leather[2] shoes, and slicked-back hair were the essentials for young men of the day. Young women in the 1950s dressed in poodle skirts and cat's-eye glasses. Miniskirts and go-go boots, worn by pop stars and fashion models of the day, were the must-haves for young women in the 1960s; the shorter the skirt, the trendier you were considered to be.

In the 1970s, both men and women wore bell-bottom pants, wide lapels,[3] and platform shoes. Designer jeans and Polo shirts were the clothing of choice for young men in the 1980s, while young women wore dresses and jackets with big shoulder pads. The late[4] Princess Diana set many fashion trends in the 1990s. The fashion world considered her to be one of the most glamorous and stylish women of the time, and newspapers would report not only on where she was and what she was doing, but also what she was wearing.

Much of the designer clothing we see models, pop stars, and other celebrities wearing is out of the price range[5] of the average shopper. In London, however, High Street stores imitate the ideas of top designers to offer the general public an inexpensive way of wearing the latest fashions. After ex-Spice Girl Geri Halliwell appeared in public wearing a dress emblazoned[6] with the Union Jack,[7] cheaper imitations of the dress, on sale in stores all over the U.K., were snapped up[8] by fashion-conscience teenage fans.

One particular style popular in the '90s was the 'retro' look. Many young people chose to dress in clothing styles of the 1960s and 1970s, or combined different elements of these past fashions with modern trends. As a result, many independent stores opened that specialized in selling old, used clothing from decades ago. Of course, there are people who adopt certain styles all the time, not just when fashion gurus[9] dictate it is appropriate. Fans of a particular type of music, for example, will always wear the clothes that match the music. The punk movement in London in the 1970s and 1980s saw many people with spiky hair, dressed in black; nowadays people who are fans of the music still adopt the same matching clothing and hair style.

Fashion is, therefore, a means of self-expression. As the British designer Katherine Hamnett said, "clothes create a wordless means of communication that we all understand." One of the first decisions that you make each day communicates a powerful statement about who you are, and what you believe in.

> 1 **catwalk** a long narrow floor that models walk along to show clothes to an audience
> 2 **patent leather** leather with a shiny finish on it
> 3 **lapel** the two pieces of cloth on the front of a coat or jacket which attach to the collar
> 4 **late** no longer alive; recently deceased
> 5 **out of one's price range** to cost more than one can afford to pay for something
> 6 **emblazoned** decorated in a very noticeable, showy way
> 7 **the Union Jack** the flag of Great Britain
> 8 **snap (something) up** to buy something quickly usually as a result of it being a bargain
> 9 **guru** used informally to talk about someone who is an expert in something; usually a spiritual teacher

Ⓑ   Read through the passage again, then answer the questions that follow.

Reading Comprehension: What Do You Remember?

Complete the sentences with the correct answer, then discuss your answers with a partner.

1. The clothes a person chooses to wear can tell others about his or her
   _____.

2. According to the reading, trends in fashion happen _____.

3. The reading mentions these four groups of people who popularize certain fashion trends: _____

4. In the 1960s, it was considered very trendy for women to wear _____
   _____, but in the '80s it was more fashionable for
   them to wear _____.

5. In the U.K., there are stores where shoppers can buy _____ versions of
   the most recent designer fashions.

6. In the 1990s, the _____ look was trendy.

7. These two British women were considered very fashionable during the 1990s:
   _____

Vocabulary Comprehension: Word Definitions

(A) Look at the vocabulary items from the reading. Write *noun*, *verb*, or *adjective* to describe each word's part of speech.

(B) For each word or phrase, write the letter of the definition in the chart.

Vocabulary	Part of Speech	Definition
1. make a statement	_____	_____
2. taste	_____	_____
3. trend	_____	_____
4. trendy	_____	_____
5. style	_____	_____
6. imitate	_____	_____
7. dictate	_____	_____
8. adopt	_____	_____
9. essential	_____	_____

a. to copy something or try to be like someone else

b. one's personal preference or liking for certain things

c. to make your opinion about something known publicly with words or actions

d. a movement; a development in how people think or act

e. something one must have

f. fashionable, in style

g. to tell, usually to order or command someone to do something

h. one's manner or way of doing something, e.g., talking or dressing

i. to choose for one's own

(C) Circle the word that best completes each statement. Then, write a sentence giving one more example for each vocabulary item.

1. In the U.S., there is a *trend* toward having (more / fewer) children per family.

2. A person with a *taste* for designer clothes would probably shop in a (discount / department) store.

3. From December through March, a (bathing suit / coat) is usually considered an *essential* item of clothing in the Northern Hemisphere.

4. If you laugh and your partner *imitates* you, he or she (laughs / frowns).

5. A (gray / red) suit would probably not be considered *trendy* by many people.

6. If someone likes your *style*, he or she likes (how you look and act / your friends and family).

7. In most countries, the (media / law) *dictates* what people can or can't do.

8. Ernest Hemmingway was originally from the U.S., but for many years he *adopted* (the U.S. / Cuba) as his home country.

9. You think wearing clothes made of animal fur is wrong. You might *make* a *statement* by (protesting in / buying from) stores that sell these clothes.

Vocabulary Skill:

The Root Word *dic/dict*

In this chapter, you read the verb 'dictate,' meaning 'to tell' or 'command.' This word is made by combining the root word 'dict' meaning 'to say,' 'tell,' or 'speak,' with the verb suffix '-ate.' 'Dict,' sometimes also written 'dic,' is combined with other root words, prefixes, and suffixes to form many words in English.

●●●

Ⓐ For each word, study the different parts. Then, write the part of speech and a simple definition. Use your dictionary to help you. Share your ideas with a partner.

Word	Part of Speech	Definition
1. dictate	_____	_____
2. dictator	_____	_____
3. diction	_____	_____
4. dictionary	_____	_____
5. contradict	_____	_____
6. indicate	_____	_____
7. predict	_____	_____
8. verdict	_____	_____

Ⓑ Complete each sentence using the words from the chart. Be sure to use the correct form of the word.

1. Can I borrow your _____ for a minute? I need to look up a word.

2. At the end of the court trial, the jury announced its _____: not guilty.

3. Brian is such a _____! He's always telling me what to do, but he never listens when I suggest an idea.

4. It's warm today, so I _____ that it will be a nice today tomorrow, too.

5. Since you don't speak Japanese, you'll have to _____ which food you want by pointing to the menu.

6. At first, Caroline said she liked the movie, but later she _____ herself and said she didn't like it very much.

7. At first it was hard to understand Spanish, but my teacher has such good _____ that I can now hear many of the sounds easily

---

Think About It | **Discuss the following questions with a partner.**

1. *Can you name any famous fashion designers from your country? Do you like the style of their designs?*

2. *Do you follow fashion trends or do you prefer to choose your own style?*

3. *Do you read fashion magazines? Which ones do you read? What do you like about them?*

4. *Is there a street or district in your city where expensive fashions are sold? Are there other places where you can buy similar fashions for much less?*

Discuss the following questions with a partner.

1. What is the difference between the two ties above? Where would a man wear each tie?

2. What do you know about the history of the tie? When and why did men begin wearing ties?

3. Why do many men today wear ties?

4. The following words and phrases can all be found in the reading. What does each mean? How is each related to topic of the reading?

wardrobe	impress	subdued
accessory	attire	

Time yourself as you read through the passage. Try to read as fluently as you can. Record your time in the Reading Rate Chart on page 202.

Make a Statement—Wear a Tie _____

One clothing item kept in almost every man's wardrobe is the tie. Wearing a tie to a social event for the first time can mark a young boy's transition[1] from youth into manhood. The wearing of a tie is also thought to transform[2] a poorly-dressed man into a well-dressed one. Many people would probably agree that the tie is *the* essential accessory to any man's shirt; what many don't realize is that the style and design can also reveal something about the character of the wearer.

5

In the seventeenth century, men in the Western world first began using

> *By focusing on general ideas while you are reading, and not on specific vocabulary, you will become a more fluent reader.*

neckwear as a clothing item. Many credit Croatia with introducing this
fashion item to the French, who later developed it into a stylish
accessory. In 1660, a group of Croatian soldiers visited Paris, which
was considered a fashion capital even at that time. In order to impress
King Louis XIV,[3] the officers paraded in front of him wearing brightly
colored silk handkerchiefs[4] around their necks. The King was so
impressed that he and many others in the royal court began wearing the
neckwear, and the use of neckties entered the world of men's fashion.

Over the centuries the style of the tie has evolved into what it is today.
Fashion designers have dictated the size of the tie which, over the years,
has varied from quite thin to very wide, as well as how the tie should
be worn. The standard width of a necktie is 82.5 millimeters; the
standard length is anywhere from 132 to 147 centimeters. After being
tied, the tie should reach the waistband of the trousers. The tie's knot
should never be so large that it can cause the collar of the shirt to open,
nor should it be too small so as to get 'lost' in the collar.

During the late 1960s and throughout the '70s, the accepted width and
length of neckties changed, with many men choosing to wear wider and
shorter ties. Fashion trends of the day allowed for ties as wide as 127
mm. The belief was that the wider tie was necessary because suit jackets
and coats had wider lapels and shirt collars were also longer. Hence, the
width and length of the tie were adjusted to match clothing trends of
the day.

Bow ties have become more popular in recent years, though they are
most often worn with dress suits[5] on very formal social occasions. Some
men consider themselves 'bow tie men' and choose to wear a bow tie
regularly instead of a straight tie. Once again, designers dictate the
acceptable dimensions[6] for a man's bow tie; it should not be broader[7]
than the widest part of a man's neck, and should not extend beyond the
outside points of the collar of his shirt.

The color of a tie can make as much of a statement as wearing a tie
itself. During the 1980s, red and yellow were considered to be the
colors of the 'power' tie; if one wanted to make a statement in business,
the color of the tie could send a message of strength and power to
colleagues and competitors. Nowadays, more subdued colors such as
blue or gray tend to be worn for business. Ties with brightly colored
designs or cartoon characters printed on them tend to be saved for
festive occasions or the office party.

The tie has now become customary attire for businessmen around the

world. For a man attending a formal meeting of any kind, the only
acceptable dress[8] would be a suit, shirt, and tie. With this simple
accessory, a man can make an important statement about who he is.

50

---

1 **transition** movement from one state of being or place to another
2 **transform** to change from one appearance to another
3 **King Louis XIV** King Louis the Fourteenth; Roman numerals are used to distinguish kings and
    queens with the same name
4 **handkerchief** a small piece of cloth used to wipe one's face or nose
5 **dress suit** formal suit, usually black, worn with a white shirt and black or white bow tie
6 **dimensions** the length and width of something
7 **broader** wider
8 **dress** clothing

Reading Comprehension: How Much Do You Remember?

(A) Choose the best answer for each question or statement below.

1. According to the reading, which of the following is NOT true about the tie?
   a. Many people feel that it is not an important clothing item to have.
   b. The tie a man wears can tell others about his style and personality.
   c. Wearing a tie for the first time is a sign of maturity for many boys.

2. The use of neckwear as a clothing accessory was introduced to the world by
   _____ soldiers in _____.
   a. French / France   **b.** French / Croatia   **c.** Croatian / France

3. According to the reading, an average necktie today is _____.
   a. about 82 mm wide   **b.** longer than 147 cm   **c.** 127 mm wide

4. During the _____, neckties were the widest.
   a. early 1960s   **b.** 1970s   **c.** 1980s

5. According to the reading, although bow ties are becoming more popular, they
   are usually only worn at _____.
   a. job interviews   **b.** formal social events   **c.** business meetings

6. If a man wears a bow tie, it should _____.
   a. be a little wider than his shirt collar
   b. not be wider than his neck
   c. be as long as it is wide

7. During the 1980s, ties of which color were worn to signal confidence or
   competitiveness in business?
   a. blue   **b.** red   **c.** gray

(B) Check your answers with a partner. Count how many you got correct—be
honest! Then, fill in the Reading Comprehension Chart on page 202.

Vocabulary Comprehension:
Word Definitions

(A) Look at the vocabulary items from the reading. Write *noun*, *verb*, or *adjective* to describe each word's part of speech.

(B) For each word or phrase, write the letter of the definition in the chart.

Vocabulary	Part of Speech	Definition
1. wardrobe	_____	_____
2. accessory	_____	_____
3. impress	_____	_____
4. evolve	_____	_____
5. adjusted	_____	_____
6. credit	_____	_____
7. occasion	_____	_____
8. attire	_____	_____
9. subdued	_____	_____

a. to develop and change, usually over a period of time

b. one's collection of clothes; also, a place in which clothes are kept

c. quiet, soft, calm

d. to cause one to feel respect, admiration, or approval for someone or something

e. changed or adapted to fit

f. something extra, usually added for decoration or comfort

g. clothing, usually formal clothes

h. to acknowledge someone for something

i. a special, often formal, event

(C) Circle the word that best completes each statement. Then, write a sentence giving one more example for each vocabulary item.

1. A common *accessory* added to many cars is (the seatbelt / a CD player).

2. Everyone is very *subdued* and there is a lot of (whispering / yelling) going on.

3. You *impress* your teacher with a paper you wrote and she gives you (an A / a D).

4. (The birth of a child / Studying for final exams) is an important *occasion* for many people.

5. Most people will have (a raincoat / an umbrella) in their winter *wardrobe*.

6. Some people believe that (humans / apes) *evolved* from (humans / apes).

7. (Jeans and a T-shirt / A suit and tie) aren't usually proper *attire* for the workplace.

8. These (pants / shoes) are too big so I have to get them *adjusted*.

9. Good (employers / employees) will give their staff *credit* for their achievements.

Vocabulary Skill:
The Use of
Dress

Ⓐ Read the paragraph below, paying attention to the underlined words and phrases.

> Hi David,
>
> You missed a great party last night! I wore that red <u>dress</u> I bought at the Be-Be boutique last week and it looked great! Jorge wore a tuxedo; he looked really handsome! The party was very festive; a lot of people were wearing the traditional <u>dress</u> of their countries. Harumi wore a Japanese kimono; Eun Mi had on a lovely Korean Hanbok—it looked rather like a long skirt with a jacket. Alec was there, and was <u>well-dressed</u> as usual; he had on quite a handsome kilt and jacket. Antonio was co-hosting the party; he was <u>dressed in</u> black from head to toe—very impressive! Kenji and his girlfriend <u>dressed up</u> in costume for the occasion—I believe they were supposed to be a king and queen, but I'm not sure. Marie came with her boyfriend Eric; she was wearing a very stylish <u>dress suit</u> and red beret, but he was completely <u>underdressed</u> in shorts, sandals, and a T-shirt! But that's Eric; he always <u>dresses down</u> like that.
>
> I'll tell you more when I see you this afternoon. I'm going to <u>get dressed</u> now then I'll drive over to your place. I'll see you in a couple of hours.
>
> Naomi

In this chapter, you've seen the word 'dress' used in different ways. Depending on its part of speech, this word can have different meanings. It can also be combined with other words to talk about one's appearance and style.

Ⓑ Match a word or phrase from the reading with a definition below. Also, write the part of speech in the chart. Check your answers with a partner.

Definition	Word or Phrase	Part of Speech
1. to put on your clothes	_____	_____
2. wearing clothes that are too informal	_____	_____
3. stylishly dressed	_____	_____
4. clothing or costume in general	_____	_____
5. an article of clothing worn by women	_____	_____
6. wearing casual clothes	_____	_____
7. to wear or be wearing	_____	_____
8. put on formal or festive clothes	_____	_____
9. formal in style	_____	_____

Ⓒ Complete the statements and questions below with one of the words or phrases from B. Then, take turns asking and answering each with a partner.

1. Describe the clothes that you are _____ right now.

2. When do you _____—before or after you eat breakfast?

3. Describe your country or culture's traditional _____. Do you ever _____ in these clothes?

4. When was the last time you _____? Was it for a special occasion?

83

What Do You Think?

Discuss the following questions with a partner.

1. *Do men in your country normally wear a suit and tie to work, or do they dress down in the workplace? Which do you prefer?*

2. *If someone looked at your wardrobe, what words would they use to describe you? Explain your answer.*

3. *What kind of clothes impress you? Describe a well-dressed man—what kind of clothes would he wear? What colors? Do the same for a woman.*

Real Life Skill

What's Your Size?

Countries all over the world have different ways of measuring clothing and shoe sizes. If you plan to visit another country, or are interested in shopping online for yourself or others, becoming familiar with some international clothing sizes can help you to make the right choices.

(A) Study the chart below. Are these ways of measuring clothes similar or identical to the measurements used in your country?

Women's Dresses/Blouses/Sweaters

	U.S.	U.K.	Europe	Japan
XS	4	8	36	5
S	6	10	38-40	7
M	8	12	42-44	9
L	10	14	46-48	11
XL	12	16	50+	13

Men's Shirt Collar

U.S./U.K.	Europe	Japan
14	36	36
$14^{1}/_{2}$	37	37
15	38	38
$15^{1}/_{2}$	39	39
16	40	40
$16^{1}/_{2}$	41	42

Women's Shoes

U.S.	U.K.	Europe	Japan
4	3	36	21.5
5	4	37	22.5
6	5	38	23.5
7	6	39	24.5
8	7	40	

Men's Shoes

U.S.	U.K.	Europe	Japan
7	6	40	24.5
8	7	41	25.5
9	8	42	26.5
10	9	43	27.5
11	10	44	

(B) Help the following people choose the right size clothes for the country they are living in. Write their measurements on the lines provided.

1. Kentaro is from Japan but he is studying in the U.K. His shirt size in Japan is 37, his shoe size 25.5. **Shirt:** _____ **Shoes:** _____

2. Birgit is from Switzerland but she is living in the U.S. Her European blouse size is 42, her shoe size is 40. **Blouse:** _____ **Shoes:** _____

3. Enrique is from Spain and he's living in the U.K. His shoe size is 43, his shirt size is 36. **Shoes:** _____ **Shirt:** _____

4. Anna is from the U.S. and is living in Japan. She needs to buy a pair of shoes. Her shoe size is 6 in the States. **Shoes:** _____

5. Simon is from London and has just moved to Tokyo. He needs to buy a new dress shirt and shoes. His U.K. measurements are shirt size $15^{1}/_{2}$ and shoe size 9. **Shirt:** _____ **Shoes:** _____

It's a Mystery

Getting Ready

Discuss the following questions with a partner.

1. *Look at the photo above. Do you know where these structures are?*
2. *Do you know of any theories about how or why these structures were made?*
3. *Do you think that ancient civilizations knew a lot about building techniques and construction?*
4. *Do you think there are some things that cannot be explained by science? If so, what are some examples?*

Before You Read:
Famous Enigmas

Discuss the following questions with a partner.

1. Are there any mysterious or unexplainable structures in your country? What are they?

2. What theories exist about how and why they were formed?

3. Look at the title of the reading. Which of the following words do you think will be in the reading passage? Why?

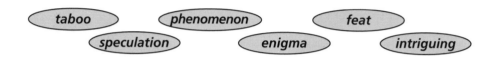

taboo   phenomenon   feat   speculation   enigma   intriguing

Reading Skill:
Identifying Main and Supporting Ideas

Every paragraph has a main idea, or topic, that tells us what the paragraph will be about. Often, you will find the main idea talked about in the first or second sentence of a paragraph. Supporting ideas usually follow the main idea. Sentences containing supporting ideas explain or give us more information about the main idea.

(A) Read the passage below and underline the sentence in each paragraph that expresses the main idea. Circle at least one supporting idea.

Earth's Mysterious Places _____

Over time, developments in archeology[1] and exploration have led to fascinating and unique discoveries. Scientists have unearthed artifacts[2] or discovered ancient cities that tell us a lot about how some of the world's oldest cultures lived. There are places on earth, though, that have puzzled
5 scientists for years and have been the subject of much discussion and speculation around the world.

Two of the most intriguing places are Easter Island and Stonehenge. Located in the South Pacific, Easter Island is one of the most isolated[3] places on earth and is famous for the large stone monoliths[4] that line its coast. These
10 structures, which were carved by ancient people to resemble human heads, range in height from about 3½ to 12 meters. Today, roughly 600 stones remain. On the opposite side of the world stands Stonehenge. This ancient English site is a collection of large stones arranged in two circles—one inside the other. Although only ruins of the original formation exist today,
15 archaeologists believe that the inner circle of bluestones, each weighing about 4 tons,[5] was built first. The giant stones that form the outer circle, known as sarsen stones, each weigh as much as 50 tons!

In South America, another mysterious phenomenon exists. Near the coast of Peru, in the high plateau of the Nazca Desert, some remarkable art is etched[6]
20 into the earth. Viewed from the ground, these etchings seem insignificant. Viewed from high above, however, these large geoglyphs, or drawings on the earth's surface, resemble birds, fish, seashells, and geometric[7] shapes. These

drawings are thought to be at least 1,500 years old, yet have remained preserved for centuries by the dry, stable climate of the desert.

Many theories exist about the ancient peoples of Easter Island, Stonehenge, and the Nazca Desert and their purposes for creating these mysterious phenomena. Archeological research suggests that Easter Island was first inhabited by Polynesians[8] around 400 A.D. Scientists believe these early inhabitants carved the island's monoliths—believed to be religious symbols—from volcanic rock, and then pulled them to their different locations.

Scientists suggest that the lines at Nazca are also related to the religious beliefs of an ancient civilization. These people believed that the mountain gods protected them by controlling the weather and the provision[9] of water. Many of the figures formed by the lines are associated with nature or water in some way. As the ancient people lived in a desert region, water was a valuable but scarce resource. Exactly how the lines were drawn without the help of aerial[10] monitoring equipment, though, remains an enigma.

Exactly how and why Stonehenge was constructed remains a mystery. Research suggests that it may have been designed and built by an ancient religious group who used it for one of two purposes; either as a sacred temple or as an observatory to study the sky. Scientists believe that the enormous stones were transported from places around the country—some up to 240 miles away—to their present site on Salisbury Plain in southern England. Work on the monument is thought to have started around 2000 B.C. and continued to 1500 B.C. Today, engineers estimate that approximately 600 people were needed to transport each sarsen stone from its point of origin to Salisbury. Scientists consider this a remarkable feat, given that heavy lifting equipment used in modern construction was not available at that time.

We may never know the exact reasons for the existence of these mysterious places. Whatever their original purposes, all three sites remain truly amazing examples of human creativity.

---

1 **archeology** /ɑrkiɑlədʒi/
2 **artifact** a man-made tool, weapon, or decoration, usually very old
3 **isolated** remote, distant, hard to reach
4 **monolith** a very large stone, often shaped in the form of a statue
5 **ton** 2,000 pounds; 1 pound = 0.45 kilograms
6 **etch** to make a picture by cutting lines into a hard surface such as metal, wood, or rock
7 **geometric** having simple, regular lines or forms
8 **Polynesians** native people of the South Pacific islands between Hawaii, New Zealand, and Easter Island
9 **provision** a stored or saved supply of something, e.g., food, water, money
10 **aerial** above ground, in the air

Ⓑ Read the statements below. Put M next to the statement that is the main idea. Put S next to the statement that is a supporting idea.

Paragraph 1

a. Scientists have found tools and other objects that tell us a lot about old cultures. _____

b. People who study the remains of ancient cultures have found many interesting things. _____

Paragraph 2

a. Easter Island and Stonehenge are two of the most interesting and unusual places on earth. _____

b. Easter Island is known best for its large statues that stand in a line along the coast. _____

Paragraph 3

a. In South America, there are ground drawings that were carved into the Nazca Desert. _____

b. There is another interesting and unusual place in South America. _____

Paragraph 4

a. Scientists have theories about why the peoples of Easter Island, the Nazca Desert, and Stonehenge created the unusual structures. _____

b. Research suggests that Easter Island's earliest people came from Polynesia. _____

Paragraph 5

a. The people of the Nazca Desert believed that mountain gods would protect them. _____

b. The art in the Nazca Desert was probably created by an ancient people for their gods. _____

Paragraph 6

a. There is disagreement about how and why Stonehenge was constructed. _____

b. Scientists are amazed that the builders of Stonehenge were able to transport the stones such long distances. _____

Reading Comprehension: What Do You Remember?

Decide if the following statements about the reading are true (*T*) or false (*F*). If you check (✔) false, correct the statement to make it true.

	T	F
1. The reading talks about three places that have puzzled scientists for years.		
2. Easter Island is located off the coast of England and has hundreds of giant stones set up in a ring.		
3. Drawings in the Nazca Desert look like animals and seashells from the ground.		
4. It is believed the structures on Easter Island were carved from volcanic rock.		
5. Scientists know how the drawings in the Nazca Desert were made.		
6. Some scientists believe that Stonehenge was used as a holy place.		
7. It probably took about 500 years to build Stonehenge.		

Ⓐ The words in *italics* are vocabulary items from the reading. Read each question or statement and choose the correct answer. Check your answers with a partner.

1. A person will most likely *resemble* his or her _____.
   a. mother or father   **b.** neighbor

2. A person studying *archeology* would probably be most interested in _____.
   a. a prehistoric weapon   **b.** a cure for a serious illness

3. Which of the following is an *enigma*?
   a. How are children born?   **b.** Is there life after death?

4. _____ is an amazing *feat*.
   a. Driving a new car   **b.** Climbing Mount Everest

5. Someone or something that is *remarkable* is _____.
   a. unusual and worth noticing **b.** typical and rather ordinary

6. Which question might most people find *intriguing*?
   a. How many planets are there in our solar system?
   b. Is there intelligent life on other planets?

7. Which might be considered an unusual *phenomenon*?
   a. the sun rising in the morning **b.** a snowstorm in summer

8. There is *speculation* that in 20 years, tourists will be able to travel to the moon. In other words, we _____ happen.
   a. know this will   **b.** believe this might

9. You are applying for a visa to enter the U.S. Which information is *insignificant*?
   a. your age   **b.** your favorite color

Ⓑ Now think of other examples using the vocabulary from A. Discuss your ideas with a partner.

1. Who else might a person *resemble*?

2. What else might a person studying *archeology* be interested in?

3. Give another example of an *enigma*.

4. Give another example of an amazing *feat*.

5. Talk about a *remarkable* place or person. Explain what makes this person or place *remarkable*.

6. Do you find the question of the existence of life on other planets *intriguing*? Why?

7. Name two *phenomena*—one natural and one unusual.

8. What else can we *speculate* about regarding the future of travel?

9. What other personal information is *insignificant* for a visa application?

Vocabulary Skill:

The Root Word *spec* + Prefixes

In this unit, you learned the word 'speculation,' meaning 'guessing about something.' This word begins with the root word 'spec,' meaning 'to observe' or 'to watch,' and is combined with the noun suffix '-tion,' meaning 'the act of.' This root (sometimes also written 'spic') is combined with prefixes and suffixes to form many words in English. When it is used with some prefixes such as 'ex-,' the spelling of the word changes.

Ⓐ Here are some common prefixes used with the root *spec*. Match the prefix with its correct meaning.

1. ex-	a. below, under
2. in-	b. forward
3. intro-	c. out, away
4. pro-	d. back, backward
5. retro-	e. within
6. sub-	f. into

Suffixes
-tion: noun
-ive: adjective

Ⓑ Look at the words below. What do you think they mean? What part of speech is each? Complete the sentences below with the correct word.

expect   suspect   inspect
prospective   introspective   retrospect

1. The police _____ Angela stole the money, but they can't prove it.

2. We _____ the plane will arrive on time; it's scheduled to come in at 3:00 this afternoon.

3. Ricardo got married at age 20, but in _____, he thinks he should have waited until he was older.

4. Carmen has two _____ buyers for her paintings. She feels certain that at least one will purchase some of her work.

5. Celine is a rather quiet and _____ young woman.

6. When I arrived in London, the customs officials opened my bags to _____ the contents.

Ⓒ Think of two more words using *spec*. Write a sentence for each. Use your dictionary to help you.

1. _____

2. _____

Think About It   Discuss the following questions with a partner.

1. *Which of the mysterious locations talked about in the reading is most intriguing to you? Why?*

2. *The reading says that it is hard to explain how the Nazca art was etched into the Peruvian desert without the use of aerial equipment. How do you think the ancient people achieved this feat?*

3. *One thousand years from now, what do you think archeologists will look at from today's society and consider unusual or mysterious? List at least two things and explain your ideas.*

Chapter 2: It's Raining Cats and Dogs, *and* Frogs!

Discuss the following questions with a partner.

1. Do you think that science can explain everything that happens in the world? Why or why not?

2. What is the meaning of the expression, 'It's raining cats and dogs'? Look at the title of the reading. Have you ever heard of an event like this?

3. Can you think of any unusual events that people cannot explain?

4. The following words are all in the reading:

inexplicable skeptic baffle
bizarre rational hoax

What does each word mean? How do you think these words relate to the topic of the reading?

Reading Skill:
Developing Reading Fluency

Time yourself as you read through the passage. Try to read as fluently as you can. Record your time in the Reading Rate Chart on page 202.

It's Raining Cats and Dogs, *and* Frogs! ____

The earth is a very weird and wonderful place. Many mysterious phenomena occur that cannot be explained by logic or science. These inexplicable events attract believers in the supernatural, as well as skeptics.

You are probably familiar with the English saying, 'It's raining cats and dogs.' Over the last 150 years, alleged instances of various animals literally raining down onto the earth have been reported. In 1861, people in Singapore reported a rain of fish following an earthquake. In 1877, several alligators fell from the sky onto a farm in the U.S. state

> *By reading fluently you will be able to read more; by reading more you will come across more new words. This will help you increase the size of your vocabulary.*

of South Carolina. Despite falling from a great height, the alligators landed on the ground unharmed. During one downpour[1] in 1966, an Australian priest was hit on the shoulder by a large fish that had fallen from the sky. The priest attempted to catch the slippery creature, but it fell into the rainwater that had flooded the ground and swam away.

The residents of the city of Naphlion in southern Greece awoke in amazement one May morning in 1981 to find small green frogs raining from the sky. The Greek Meteorological[2] Institute concluded that the frogs had been picked up by strong winds and transported in storm clouds. When the clouds broke and the rain came down, so did the frogs. What is most interesting about this story is that the frogs were discovered to be a species native to North Africa! A more recent example of nature's amazing feats took place in the summer of 2000 in Ethiopia when millions of fish, some dead and some alive, reportedly rained down from the sky.

While both scientists and skeptics seek rational explanations for these bizarre instances, some events have left them baffled. One such incident happened in France in 1814. In September of that year, on a clear day, a small, spherical[3] cloud was spotted floating in the sky. Witnesses say that the cloud hovered[4] before spinning and moving quickly in a southerly direction. A deafening noise was then heard coming from the cloud, which then suddenly exploded in a shower of rocks and stones.

Today, there are a record[5] number of stories about phenomena that cannot be explained by science or logic. Magazines, journals, and websites have been created to share information with the public about inexplicable happenings such as strange lights and weird noises. While many of the events recorded in these publications have been dismissed[6] as hoaxes, some remain outside the scope of scientific explanation. Two of the most controversial phenomena are crop circles and spontaneous human combustion.

Crop circles are very large, ornate[7] designs that seem to appear overnight in wheat and corn fields, usually during spring and summer. This phenomenon made headlines all over the world in the 1990s, but whether it is a natural phenomenon or simply a hoax remains unknown. The phenomenon of spontaneous human combustion—in which a person suddenly catches fire for no apparent reason—also has yet to be given a rational explanation. Numerous examples of this phenomenon have been recorded, and its causes have even been investigated by the FBI.[8] Most experts believe that it must be connected with some kind of chemical reaction inside the body. However, although there are theories on how and why it can happen, a satisfactory explanation has yet to be found.

We live on a planet full of mystery and wonder. Stories of bizarre events are circulated via the Internet, TV, and other media. Some are true, others are hoaxes, but all are weird and, one could argue, wonderful!

---

1 **downpour** very heavy rain
2 **meteorological** related to the scientific study of the weather
3 **spherical** /sfɪrəkəl/ shaped like a round ball
4 **hover** to float or stay in the air above something, usually for a period of time
5 **record** a larger number of something than ever before noted
6 **dismiss** to reject
7 **ornate** decorative
8 **FBI** Federal Bureau of Investigation, a governmental police department in the U.S.

Reading Comprehension: How Much Do You Remember?

Ⓐ For each question or statement below, choose the correct answer.

1. Stories about unusual events often attract _____.
   a. believers   **b.** disbelievers   **c.** both a and b

2. Which of the following does the reading NOT talk about?
   a. people catching fire   **b.** visitors from other planets
   c. unusual shapes in wheat and corn fields

3. _____ fell from the sky onto people in Singapore in the mid-nineteenth century.
   a. Alligators   **b.** Fish   **c.** Frogs

4. What was unusual about the animals that rained down on the Greek city of Naphlion?
   a. They were yellow.   **b.** They were extremely large.
   c. They had come from another country.

5. According to the reading, today there are _____ about unexplained phenomena.
   a. more stories than ever   **b.** fewer stories   **c.** hardly any stories

6. Most of the unusual events documented on websites and in the media _____.
   a. have been proven false   **b.** are difficult for scientists to explain
   c. are now being studied by the FBI

7. In the 1990s, stories about _____ appeared in newspapers around the world.
   a. crop circles   **b.** raining fish
   c. an unusual earthquake

Ⓑ Check your answers with a partner. Count how many you got correct—be honest! Then, fill in the Reading Comprehension Chart on page 202.

Vocabulary Comprehension:
Odd Word Out

(A) For each group, circle the word that does not belong. The words in *italics* are vocabulary items from the reading.

1. *inexplicable*	mysterious	puzzling	understandable
2. disbeliever	doubter	believer	*skeptic*
3. trick	*hoax*	fraud	truth
4. *bizarre*	strange	typical	weird
5. *rational*	unreasonable	irrational	illogical
6. informed	confused	*baffled*	puzzled
7. supposed	definite	suspected	*alleged*
8. event	*instance*	series	situation
9. *scope*	partial	range	realm

(B) Complete the sentences using the words in *italics* from A. Be sure to use the correct form of the word.

1. Andrew isn't a very _____ person; he lets his emotions control him too much.

2. Tony understands a little bit about computers, but programming is outside his _____ of knowledge.

3. Someone called the radio station this morning to say the president had died, but later, we learned it was only a _____.

4. I've tried to understand this math problem all afternoon, but I can't. I'm _____!

5. If you want Seok Chan to believe that you saw a ghost, you'll have to prove it. He's a _____ and won't believe it until he sees for himself.

6. Can you think of an _____ when it is okay to tell a lie?

7. Well, that's _____. I'm quite sure I left my keys on the table, but now they're gone.

8. The police are speaking to the man about his _____ involvement in the robbery.

9. Carlos insists he heard someone breaking into the house. As the police cannot find any evidence, his story is _____.

Vocabulary Skill:

The Root Word *scop* + Prefixes

Ⓐ Study the chart, then add *scope* to each prefix to form words that match the definitions.

Prefix	Meaning
tele-	at a distance
micro-	small
peri-	around
horo-	hour
stetho-	chest

One might use a ...	
1.	to listen to your heart.
2.	to predict your future using your date of birth.
3.	to study organisms impossible to see with the eye alone, such as bacteria or cells.
4.	to study the planets or other heavenly bodies.
5.	to see something under water.

> In Chapter 1, you learned that the root word 'spec' means 'to observe' or 'to watch.' In this chapter, you learned the word 'scope,' which comes from the root word 'scop,' also meaning 'to observe' or 'to look at.' 'Scope' can be used alone or combined with prefixes and suffixes to form many words in English.

Ⓑ Complete the sentences below using the information from the chart in A. Begin each sentence using a word from the list below.

(astrologer)   (doctor)   (sailor)   (biologist)   (astronomer)

1. A(n) _____ might use a _____
   to _____.
2. A(n) _____ to _____
   _____.
3. A(n) _____ to _____
   _____.
4. A(n) _____
   _____.
5. A(n) _____
   _____.

Ⓒ Now write three sentences of your own using some of the words in A. Share your ideas with a partner.

1. _____
2. _____
3. _____

What Do You Think?

Discuss the following questions with a partner.

1. *Can you think of any rational explanations for spontaneous human combustion or crop circles?*

2. *Do you know of any unusual phenomena that were found to be hoaxes?*

3. *In general, do you consider yourself to be a believer in or a skeptic of mysterious phenomena? Explain your answer.*

4. *Have you, or has anyone you know, ever been involved in a mysterious or unusual incident? What happened? Was there a rational explanation for the event?*

Real Life Skill

Reading Advertisements

In this unit, you read about many different types of unusual and mysterious happenings. In newspapers, magazines, and on TV, it's common to see advertisements offering a variety of services to help people understand mysterious life events or to predict the future.

Ⓐ Read the advertisements below, paying particular attention to the words in bold. What do the words mean? Write a short definition next to each box. Use your dictionary to help you.

1.
The **Zodiac** Hotline is here to help! **Astrologers** available to give your **horoscope** 24 hours a day! *Don't wait. Call now!* *First minute is FREE. $2.50. per minute thereafter. 555-6782*

_____
_____
_____

2.
Fortunetellers Village **Palm readers** and **numerologists** available from 9–5 weekdays. $35 an hour. Call Angel (555-9828) for a free consultation.

_____
_____
_____

Ⓑ For each situation below, which of the services above would you use? In some cases, more than one answer is possible.

Situation	Contact
1. You want to know if you and your boy or girlfriend are right for each other based on your date and time of birth.	
2. You want to know more about your personality based on your sun, moon, and rising signs.	
3. You want to know if you're going to get into your university of choice.	

Ⓒ Would you ever use either of the services above? Why? What would you want to find out?

The Future of Medicine

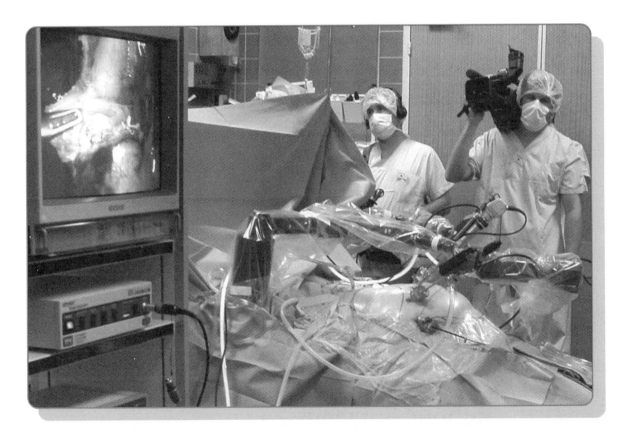

Getting Ready

Discuss the following questions with a partner.

1. *Look at the photo above. What is happening? Where is it happening? What kind of instruments are being used?*
2. *Is this what you would usually expect to see in an operating room?*
3. *What is a robot? Can you think of ways that a robot could be used in a hospital?*
4. *In what ways has the field of medicine and medical technology changed in recent years?*

Before You Read:

Future Surgery

Ⓐ Read the sentences below.

1. A doctor makes long *incisions*.
2. A doctor makes long *incisions* in a patient's chest.
3. A doctor makes long *incisions* in a patient's chest to reach the heart.

Which sentence best helped you to understand the meaning of the word *incision*? Explain your answer to a partner.

Ⓑ Find each italicized word in the reading below. Read the sentence in which the word appears and some of the surrounding sentences. Then choose the best definition.

1. In line 3, the phrase *make-believe* means
   a. realistic   **b.** imaginary   **c.** uncertain

2. In line 9, the word *trauma* means a
   a. difficult work   **b.** great sadness   **c.** physical injury or wound

3. In line 19, the word *inserted* means
   a. put in   **b.** removed   **c.** cut

4. In line 22, the word *relays* means
   a. creates   **b.** lights up   **c.** sends

Reading Skill:

Identifying Meaning from Context

> To guess the meaning of an important but unfamiliar word in a reading passage, try the following: First, think about how the new word is related to the topic of the reading. Second, identify what part of speech the word is. Third, look at the words surrounding the new word for synonyms, antonyms, or an explanation of the word.

Ⓐ Read the passage below. Pay attention to the words *invasive, console, counterintuitive,* and *mimic*. Use the context of the sentences, the topic, the part of speech, and the surrounding words to guess the meaning of the words.

Robotic Surgeons _____

Images of robotic equipment being used in operating rooms were once seen only in science-fiction movies. Today, the use of robotic equipment for certain types of surgery is no longer make-believe—it's real!

Traditional surgical procedures[1] require surgeons to make large
5 incisions in a patient's body in order to gain access to the internal organs.[2] It was once common for heart surgeons, who perform highly specialized and complex procedures, to make long incisions in a patient's chest and then split the breastbone to reach the heart. The patient then had to recover from the trauma of the surgical treatment,
10 the split bone, *and* the large wound created by the incision. Patients who undergo surgery requiring this kind of invasive procedure are often prone[3] to infection,[4] as bacteria can infect the cut in the skin. In addition, there is often a lengthy recovery period.

A surgical technique known as 'keyhole surgery' has become more common in recent years. This technique eliminates the need for surgeons to make large incisions. Instead, a couple of small incisions, each measuring about one centimeter, are made around the area to be operated on. Long instruments, which look a bit like chopsticks, are inserted through the tiny incisions and into the patient's body. At the end of these instruments are small tools that resemble standard surgical tools. A tiny camera, called an endoscope, is also inserted into the body through one of the incisions. The camera relays an image of what is happening inside the patient's body to a large computer monitor, so doctors are able to see what is going on, and where to place the tools. The awkward part of keyhole surgery is that it is counterintuitive; if a surgeon wants to move the tool to the left, he or she must push it to the right, and vice versa.

Other advancements in technology are also being used today in the OR.[5] A new machine called the da Vinci™ Surgical System has been tested in hospitals in the U.S. This robotic apparatus[6] requires that surgeons make three small incisions in the body. Two of the slits are for instruments; the third is for the endoscope. Unlike keyhole surgery, the da Vinci™ robot's moving parts are designed to mimic the natural hand and wrist movements of a surgeon, thus providing better control and sensitivity. Sitting at a console a few feet from a patient, the surgeon can perform an operation by holding and moving highly sensitive pads that enable him or her to control the instruments. The area of the body on which the surgeon is working is magnified[7] on a screen, which is attached to the console. This gives surgeons a realistic three-dimensional view of the area—similar to what they would see during a traditional surgical procedure.

Although the da Vinci™ Surgical System is undergoing trials for some procedures, it has been hailed as revolutionary by many surgeons. Patients with serious illnesses must still undergo major surgery, but the smaller incisions and less invasive procedures typically mean that there is less physical trauma to the body, so a shorter recovery time is needed. In some cases, the patients' stay in the hospital has been cut in half when the da Vinci™ Surgical System was used. On the downside, some operations have taken up to fifty minutes longer because surgeons are inexperienced at using the new technology. As surgeons become more familiar with the machines, the time needed for surgical procedures is likely to decrease.

As technologies continue to develop in the medical field, we may find that robots become a permanent feature of the OR.

> 1 **procedure** a specific way of doing something
> 2 **internal organs** parts inside the body, e.g. heart, liver, kidneys, etc.
> 3 **prone (to)** easily affected by, or having a tendency toward something
> 4 **infection** an illness caused when small organisms, such as bacteria or a virus, enter the body
> 5 **OR** operating room
> 6 **apparatus** a tool or piece of equipment used for a specific purpose
> 7 **magnified** enlarged

Ⓑ Now read the passage again, and answer the questions that follow.

Reading Comprehension: What Do You Remember?

How much do you remember from the reading? Read each question or statement below and choose the correct answer.

1. Traditional surgical procedures often leave _____ in a person's body.
   a. a tiny cut   **b.** a large wound   **c.** a dangerous infection

2. Many patients who have heart surgery have difficulty after the operation because _____.
   a. they cannot eat for days   **b.** the incision becomes infected
   c. the cost of the surgery is very high

3. Which of the following is NOT true of keyhole surgery?
   a. It can be quite an invasive procedure.
   b. It requires the use of long, thin tools and a small camera.
   c. A doctor views the inside of a patient's body on a computer screen.

4. What is one disadvantage of keyhole surgery?
   a. It makes a patient's body look very large on the monitor.
   b. The direction in which a doctor moves the surgical tools is reversed.
   c. An endoscope has to be inserted into the patient's body.

5. The da Vinci™ Surgical System differs from keyhole surgery in that it _____.
   a. requires the use of small tools and a camera inside the patient's body
   b. allows the surgeon to use the surgical instruments in a more intuitive way
   c. requires that a surgeon make more incisions in the patient's body

6. What is the main benefit of using keyhole surgery and the da Vinci™ Surgical System?
   a. There is less trauma to the body and, therefore, people recover faster.
   b. Both reduce the amount of time it takes to perform a surgical procedure.
   c. Fewer doctors are needed to perform surgery on a patient.

7. At the moment, the da Vinci™ Surgical System and keyhole surgery are _____ common in the U.S.
   a. very   **b.** somewhat   **c.** not at all

Ⓐ The words in *italics* are vocabulary items from the reading. Read each question or statement and choose the correct answer. Check your answers with a partner.

1. Which of the following is *make-believe*?
   a. the moon   **b.** Santa Claus

2. You would *insert* a _____ an envelope.
   a. letter into   **b.** stamp onto

3. In the U.S., people drive on the right side of the road. It's *counterintuitive* to drive on the _____ side.
   a. right   **b.** left

4. If you smile, and someone *mimics* you, that person _____.
   a. also smiles   **b.** frowns at you

5. Many people would consider _____ *invasive*.
   a. opening a door for someone else
   b. opening and reading someone else's mail

6. Which of the following would you *relay*?
   a. a message   **b.** a computer

7. If you make an *incision* in the skin, you make a _____ cut.
   a. small   **b.** deep and wide

8. If a person suffers head *trauma*, he or she may _____.
   a. have a headache   **b.** be unconscious

9. Which of the following typically appears on a stereo *console*?
   a. a volume control   **b.** CD player

Ⓑ Now think of other examples using the vocabulary from A. Discuss your ideas with a partner.

1. Name something else that is *make-believe*.
2. What else might you *insert* in an envelope?
3. In your country, is it *counterintuitive* to drive on the left or the right side of the road?
4. Do something now that *mimics* your partner.
5. What is something else people might consider *invasive*?
6. How could you *relay* a message?
7. Has a doctor ever made an *incision* in your skin? For what purpose?
8. Have you, or has someone you know, ever suffered physical *trauma*?
9. What else might you find on a stereo *console*?

Vocabulary Skill:
Homonyms

In this chapter, you read the noun 'console.' The verb form of this word has different syllable stress than the noun form, and it has a different meaning. Words such as this, with identical spellings but different meanings and pronunciation are called homonyms. They can easily cause confusion when you are reading. One helpful strategy is to pay attention to the part of speech of the word in the sentence.

Ⓐ Practice saying both the noun and verb forms of the word *console*. The stress in each is on the underlined part of the word. Then, read the two sentences below and decide which part of speech is being used. Write *noun* or *verb* on the line.

Ⓑ Using the sentences to help you, write a simple definition for the verb form of *console*.

> <u>con</u>sole /kɑnsoʊl/ *n* a panel which contains the controls used to run a machine, e.g., a computer or stereo
>
> con<u>sole</u> /kənsoʊl/ *v*

1. _____ When Eun Mi failed her test, Seong Won tried to *console* her.
2. _____ To control the image on the screen, press different buttons on the computer *console*.

Ⓒ Now, do the same for each of the word pairs below. Compare your answers with a partner.

> <u>pro</u>ject /prɑdʒɛkt/ *n* a task that someone works on
>
> pro<u>ject</u> /prədʒɛkt/ *v* _____

1. _____ Are you working on the presentation alone, or is it a group *project*?
2. _____ Some medical specialists *project* that we'll soon find a cure for cancer.

> <u>com</u>plex /kɑmplɛks/ *n* _____
>
> com<u>plex</u> /kəmplɛks/ *adj* complicated, not easy to do or understand

3. _____ The shopping *complex* nearby has stores that sell many different things—clothes, food, household appliances.
4. _____ I took calculus last semester but didn't do very well. It was just too *complex* for me.

Ⓓ Practice saying the sentences from C with your partner. Pay attention to the pronunciation of the word pairs.

Think About It | **Discuss the following questions with a partner.**

1. *Do you think that robotic instruments make surgery safer or more dangerous?*
2. *How do you think medicine and medical technology will change in the future?*
3. *What other types of medical treatment do people in your country use to stay healthy or to deal with illness or pain?*

Discuss the following questions with a partner.

1. List four uses of the Internet.

2. How might the Internet be useful to people in the medical field and to those who need medical care?

3. Where is Antarctica? What do you know about this place?

4. The following words are all in the reading passage:

anticipate   inaccessible   ailing
atmosphere   improvise

What does each word mean? Look at the title of the reading passage. How do you think each word relates to the topic of the reading?

Time yourself as you read through the passage. Try to read as fluently as you can. Record your time in the Reading Rate Chart on page 202.

Reading Skill:
Developing Reading Fluency

Building vocabulary will help you read more fluently. When you know more words, you can read faster and with more confidence. Work on building your vocabulary all the time—not just in reading class.

Internet Rescue _____

Jerri Nielsen, a physician from Ohio, has the Internet to thank for saving her life. When she accepted a job in Antarctica as the only doctor at the Amundsen-Scott South Pole Station, she could never have anticipated how technology would help her.

Antarctica is the most isolated place on earth. Every year, scientists from all over the world travel there to work in conditions of extreme cold, with temperatures reaching minus 100 degrees Fahrenheit. In addition to being cold, the atmosphere is extremely dry and windy.

5

Between February and October each year it gets so cold that parts of the continent are inaccessible. Around the middle of the continent, near the South Pole Station, the cold weather causes plane fuel to change consistency,[1] making it impossible for aircraft to land. Thus, between February and October, the team of researchers at the station must live together in isolation.

Numerous research stations exist on Antarctica, and staff may need medical treatment for anything from a cold to a bad cut. The extreme cold, wind, and dryness of the Antarctic environment can also cause many ailments. Hence, at each of the research stations, a doctor must be on call twenty-four hours a day, seven days a week. When Jerri Nielsen saw an ad in a medical journal for doctors to work at the U.S. Antarctic research base, she was interested. She applied for the job, talked things over with her family, and decided to go. By November 1998, Jerri was settling into her new home for the year—an orange metal shack in Antarctica, which also doubled as her clinic.

Jerri had previously practiced emergency medicine only in the sterile confines of a hospital. For the next few months, she experienced a totally different working environment. She discovered that the weather played havoc with[2] conventional treatments—adhesive bandages would not stick, and wounds took longer to heal. As a result, Jerri found it necessary to improvise and think of new ways to care for her patients. Jerri also found herself looking at relationships with her patients in a new light.[3] She was the only doctor to a group of forty people, and unlike in the U.S., her patients became her friends.

In March 1999, a few weeks after the last flight until November had left the station, Jerri felt a hard lump in her right breast. She kept it secret from her colleagues, but during the following months the lump grew in size. In June, she decided to inform her supervisor. Two days later, after exchanging e-mails with the Denver-based doctor in charge of the Antarctic medical programs, a colleague helped Jerri perform initial[4] tests. Using only ice to numb the area, a needle was inserted into the lump in an attempt to draw out[5] fluid. When no fluid came out, Jerri knew the lump was cancerous.

Over the next few months, Jerri relied on e-mails from doctors in the U.S. for medical support, and from her family for moral support.

Necessary medical supplies and cancer-fighting drugs were successfully airdropped and Jerri, with the help of her colleagues, began treatment to fight the disease. On October 16, 1999, seven months after discovering the lump, Jerri and another ailing colleague were picked up from the South Pole, and a replacement physician was dropped off. `50`

Jerri had the lump removed back in the U.S. Medical tests showed that the cancer had not spread to other parts of her body. Thanks to the Internet, Jerri made it home alive and, in 2001, published a book about her remarkable experience. `55`

---

1 **consistency** the physical nature of something; how thick, thin, hard, soft, etc. something is
2 **play havoc with (something)** to disrupt or upset something
3 **look at something in a new light** to think about something in a new or different way
4 **initial** first
5 **draw out** to remove, to take out

Reading Comprehension: How Much Do You Remember?

(A) Decide if the following statements about the reading are true (*T*) or false (*F*). If you check (✔) false, correct the statement to make it true.

	T	F
1. Jerri Nielsen is an American doctor who lived in Antarctica for almost a year.		
2. Between February and October, warmer weather in Antarctica makes the South Pole Station accessible by aircraft.		
3. According to the reading, wounds heal more quickly in Antarctica than they do in warmer countries.		
4. Prior to working in Antarctica, Jerri worked in an emergency room.		
5. In June 1999, Jerri discovered she had breast cancer.		
6. Until she returned to the U.S., Jerri had almost no contact with other doctors or her family.		
7. Jerri left Antarctica in October 1999 and returned to the U.S. with a sick coworker.		

(B) Check your answers with a partner. Count how many you got correct—be honest! Then, fill in the Reading Comprehension Chart on page 202.

Vocabulary Comprehension: Odd Word Out

Ⓐ For each group, circle the word that does not belong. The words in *italics* are vocabulary items from the reading.

1. *anticipate*	expect	be certain	suppose
2. surroundings	environment	inside	*atmosphere*
3. available	*inaccessible*	unreachable	remote
4. *on call*	available	on hand	absent
5. different	typical	*conventional*	usual
6. infected	*sterile*	dirty	polluted
7. prepare	make up	invent	*improvise*
8. help	*moral support*	opposition	encouragement
9. *ailing*	ill	well	sick

Ⓑ Complete the sentences using the words in *italics* from A. Be sure to use the correct form of the word.

1. For her wedding, Emily chose not to wear a _____ white dress. Instead, she wore a purple dress with a white hat.

2. I didn't _____ that so many people would attend the meeting, so I only set out fifty chairs.

3. Dr. Kim isn't in her office, but she is _____ until midnight. You can phone or page her until then.

4. Don't worry if you haven't memorized your speech. If you forget something, just _____, and say something else.

5. My grandmother had a heart attack two months ago, and she's been _____ ever since.

6. The _____ in the classroom was so hot that it made it impossible to concentrate.

7. Jasmine was so nervous about going to the doctor that her sister went along to offer _____.

8. All of the surgical instruments must be _____ in order to avoid infecting the patient.

9. You'll have to walk the last mile to reach the cabin. It's _____ by car.

The Prefixes *ante-*, *pro-*, and *post-*

A What do you think the following words mean? Use them to complete the sentences below.

> **prognosis**   **anterior**   **prologue**
>
> **postpone**   **posterior**

1. I'm afraid I'm going to have to _____ my doctor's appointment again. Can I reschedule for next week?

2. Before you begin reading the story, please read the author's _____ on pages 1–3.

3. The doctor says that Jim's _____ is good. The cancer hasn't spread, and eventually he should make a full recovery.

4. According to brain research, the frontal lobes of the brain function differently. The _____ part enables us to understand humor, while the back, or _____ part, helps us to move our bodies.

B Now use either *ante-*, *pro-*, or *post-* to complete the sentences below. Check answers with a partner.

1. If you're planning to travel tonight in the rain, please ____ceed with caution. The roads are very slippery.

2. It is common knowledge now that some women suffer from ____natal depression after giving birth.

3. Fashions of the mid-twentieth century are the ____cedents of many of today's clothing styles.

4. Do you believe ____phecies that say in 100 years, the world will end?

5. Today is March 1, but my paycheck is ____dated to March 10. Is there some mistake?

6. Fumiko and Kotaro attended ____natal classes in the months before the birth of their first child.

> In this chapter, you learned the word 'anticipate,' meaning 'to expect' or 'to think something will happen.' This word begins with the prefix 'ant(e)-,' meaning 'in front of' or 'before.' The prefix 'pro-' also means 'before' or 'forward.' The prefix 'post-' means 'after.' Many words in English are formed by combining these prefixes with root words, nouns, verbs, and adjectives.

What Do You Think?

Discuss the following questions with a partner.

1. *How do you think Jerri had to improvise while in Antarctica? Talk about a time that you had to improvise.*

2. *Imagine that it's July 1999 and you've just read a newspaper article about Jerri's situation in Antarctica. Write an e-mail to her offering your moral support. Share your e-mail with a partner.*

Real Life Skill

Common Medical Abbreviations

In this unit, you read the abbreviation 'OR,' meaning 'Operating Room.' There are many common medical abbreviations used to refer to doctors, places in a hospital, tools used by health specialists, and one's health. These abbreviations are written as well as said, and when spoken, each letter of the abbreviation is pronounced.

Ⓐ Practice saying the abbreviations. Then, match each abbreviation to its correct meaning.

1. OR	**a.** intensive care unit
2. MD	**b.** operating room
3. IV	**c.** deoxyribonucleic acid
4. CPR	**d.** blood pressure
5. HIV	**e.** emergency room
6. OB-GYN	**f.** medical doctor
7. ER	**g.** human immunodeficiency virus
8. ICU	**h.** obstetrician-gynecologist
9. DNA	**i.** intravenous injection
10. BP	**j.** cardiopulmonary resuscitation

Ⓑ Complete each sentence below with the appropriate abbreviation from A. Check your answers with a partner.

1. A person in a car accident will probably be brought here upon reaching the hospital. _____

2. If a person is seriously injured, after surgery, he will probably go from the OR to this place in the hospital. _____

3. You'd see this doctor if you were going to have a child. _____

4. You might see this physician once a year for a check up. _____

5. This causes the disease AIDS. _____

6. If you were unable to drink or eat in a hospital, you might get one of these. _____

7. This is the genetic material that determines what you will look like. _____

8. This shouldn't be higher than 140 over 90. If it is, you may suffer from hypertension. _____

9. A man on the bus collapses and stops breathing. You might do this and save his life. _____

Journey into Space

Getting Ready

Discuss the following questions with a partner.

1. *Use the words below to describe what is happening in the picture above.*

astronaut   space   manned   journey   gravity

2. *How much do you know about the history of space travel?*

3. *Is there a space agency in your country? What projects is the agency involved in?*

4. *Make three predictions about the future of space travel.*

Before You Read:
Astronaut Activities

Discuss the following questions with a partner.

1. What do you know about the job of an astronaut? What kind of work does an astronaut do in space?

2. What do you think makes the job of an astronaut interesting? What makes it challenging?

3. The following words can all be found in the reading:

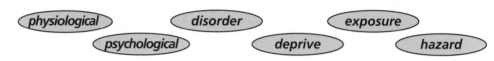

physiological   disorder   exposure

psychological   deprive   hazard

What does each word mean? How does each relate to the topic of the reading?

Reading Skill:
Identifying Main and Supporting Ideas

Every paragraph has a main idea, or topic, that tells us what that paragraph is about. Often, you will find the main idea talked about in the first or second sentence of a paragraph. Supporting ideas usually follow the main idea. Sentences containing supporting ideas explain or give us more information about the main idea.

Ⓐ Read the passage below and underline the sentence in each paragraph that expresses the main idea. Circle at least one supporting idea.

The Challenges of Space Travel _____

For centuries, humans have looked up at the sky and wondered what exists beyond the realm of our planet. Ancient astronomers examined the night sky hoping to learn more about the universe. More recently, movies such as Stanley Kubrick's *2001: A Space Odyssey* explored the possibility of
5 sustaining human life in outer space, while other films have questioned whether extraterrestrial life forms may have visited our planet.

Since astronaut Yuri Gagarin became the first man to travel in space in 1961, scientists have researched what conditions are like beyond Earth's atmosphere, and what effects space travel has on the human body.
10 Although most astronauts do not spend more than a few months in space, many experience physiological and psychological problems when they return to Earth. Some of these ailments are short-lived; others may be long-lasting.

More than two-thirds of all astronauts suffer from motion sickness while
15 traveling in space. In the gravity-free environment, the body cannot distinguish up from down. The body's internal balance system sends confusing signals to the brain, which can result in nausea[1] lasting as long as a few days. A body that is deprived of gravity also experiences changes in the distribution of bodily fluids. More fluid than normal ends up in the
20 face, neck, and chest, resulting in a puffy face, bulging neck veins, and a slightly enlarged heart.

Throughout the duration of a mission, astronauts' bodies experience some potentially dangerous disorders. One of the most common is loss of muscle mass and bone density. Another effect of the weightless environment is that astronauts tend not to use their legs as much, so the muscles gradually atrophy.[2] This, combined with the shift of fluid to the upper body and the resulting loss of essential minerals such as calcium, causes bones to weaken. Bone density can decrease at a rate of 1 to 2 percent a month and, as a result, many astronauts are unable to walk properly for a few days upon their return to earth. Exposure to radiation[3] is another serious hazard that astronauts face. Without the earth's atmosphere to protect them, astronauts can be exposed to intense radiation from the sun and other galactic bodies,[4] leaving them at risk of cancer.

In addition to physiological difficulties, astronauts who travel for extended periods may also suffer from psychological stress. Astronauts live and work in small, tight spaces, and they must be able to deal both physically and mentally with the confined environment. In addition, long periods away from family and friends can leave space travelers feeling lonely and depressed.

Now that man has been to the Moon and unmanned missions have been sent to Mars, many believe that the next major step in space travel will be a manned mission to and from Mars. Differences between the orbits[5] of Earth and Mars mean that such a mission would take almost three years to complete. The National Space Biomedical Research Institute (NSBRI) is currently investigating whether such an operation is possible in light of the hazards astronauts face. During short missions, some of the physical and mental challenges of space travel can be controlled with diet and regular exercise. In the case of long-term space travel, however, it is still not entirely clear if the human body could adapt and survive.

In 2010, the NSBRI is due to present its findings to NASA[6] and present a 'go' or 'no go' recommendation regarding a manned mission to Mars. As new technologies develop to help scientists further pursue their goals, we may one day see humans walk on distant planets.

---

[1] **nausea** a feeling of sickness that may cause one to vomit
[2] **atrophy** to become weak, to lose size and strength
[3] **radiation** heat or light from something such as the sun, a microwave, or x-rays that can be harmful to humans
[4] **galactic bodies** other stars and planets in the galaxy
[5] **orbit** the curved path that a planet or space shuttle makes around a star or another planet
[6] **NASA** National Aeronautics and Space Administration; the agency in the U.S. that is responsible for space exploration and travel

Ⓑ Read the statements below. Put M next to the statement that is the main idea. Put S next to the statement that is a supporting idea.

Paragraph 1

a. In ancient times, scientists looked at the sky to learn about the universe. _____

b. For many years, people have looked up at the sky and wondered about space. _____

Paragraph 2

a. Astronauts often suffer from physical and mental difficulties related to space travel. _____

b. Scientists today are very interested in how space travel can affect the human body. _____

Paragraph 3

a. An upset stomach is one of the disorders many astronauts suffer from in space. _____

b. The gravity-free environment can cause astronauts to suffer from other ailments. _____

Paragraph 4

a. During a space mission, astronauts face conditions that endanger their health. _____

b. During a space mission, astronauts may suffer from loss of muscle mass and bone density. _____

Paragraph 5

a. Long-term space travel can be mentally and physically stressful for many astronauts. _____

b. During space travel, astronauts may have difficulty adjusting to a small, uncomfortable living and working environment. _____

Paragraph 6

a. The next major development in manned space travel may be a trip to the planet Mars. _____

b. A return trip to Mars would probably take about three years. _____

Reading Comprehension:
What Do You Remember?

Decide if the following statements about the reading are true (*T*) or false (*F*). If you check (✔) false, correct the statement to make it true.

	T	F
1. In 1961, the first astronaut traveled to space.		
2. As a result of weightlessness, astronauts' legs and arms are often swollen with fluid.		
3. One of the dangers of space travel is that an astronaut's bones and muscles may become weaker because of the weight of the space suit.		
4. Another danger that astronauts face in space is prolonged contact with cancerous rays from the sun.		
5. During short-term space travel, many astronauts can maintain their physical and mental health with simple exercise and proper food.		
6. Many scientists feel certain that humans could endure a three-year journey in space.		
7. The NSBRI has okayed a manned mission to Mars.		

(A) The words in *italics* are vocabulary items from the reading. Read each question or statement and choose the correct answer. Compare your answers with a partner.

1. Ryuichi says, "Physics is outside my *realm* of knowledge." In other words, he _____ this subject very well.
   a. understands   b. doesn't understand

2. Which is an example of a *physiological* problem?
   a. poor eyesight   b. depression

3. _____ would be considered a *psychological* problem.
   a. Fear of flying   b. Coughing

4. It's often hard to *distinguish* between _____.
   a. mother and daughter   b. identical twins

5. In which setting might you be *deprived* of water?
   a. a beach   b. a desert

6. If there is an even *distribution* of wealth in a country, there is a _____ number of very rich and very poor people.
   a. large   b. small

7. To protect your skin from *exposure* to the sun, you should wear _____.
   a. a bathing suit   b. sun screen

8. Most people would agree that _____ is a *hazard* to your health.
   a. smoking   b. exercising

9. A person with an eating *disorder* eats _____ food.
   a. just the right amount of b. too little or too much

(B) Now think of other examples using the vocabulary from A. Share your ideas with a partner.

1. Name a subject that is outside your *realm* of knowledge.
2. Give another example of a *physiological* problem.
3. How might someone overcome the *psychological* problem of fear of spiders?
4. What could you do to *distinguish* between two people who look alike?
5. Where else might you be *deprived* of water?
6. Is there an even *distribution* of wealth in your country?
7. How else can you protect your skin from *exposure* to the sun?
8. Give another example of a health *hazard*. Explain why it is *hazardous*.
9. Give an example of another type of physiological or psychological *disorder*.

Vocabulary Skill:

The Prefixes
dis- and *de-*

In this chapter, you learned the word 'deprived,' meaning 'without something that is necessary;' you also read the noun 'disorder,' meaning 'an illness,' or 'something that is not in order.' The prefix 'de-' means 'reduce,' 'remove,' or 'not.' 'Dis-' also means 'not,' as well as 'apart.' These are two very common prefixes that come before nouns, verbs, adjectives, and adverbs to form many words in English.

A What do you think the following words mean? Complete the sentences below using the words.

> deduct   detach   discharge
> depart   disgrace

1. At what time is our plane scheduled to _____?

2. The Olympic athlete faced public _____ after it was discovered he'd taken drugs in order to win the competition.

3. When you hand in your application, _____ and return the lower part of the document. Keep the upper part for your records.

4. After serving in the military for two years, Jin Ho received an honorable _____ from the army.

5. If you turn your test paper in late, Professor Yeo will _____ ten points from your score.

B Now use either *de-* or *dis-* to complete the sentences below. Use your dictionary to help you.

1. The plane is about to make its _____scent into Tokyo. We should be arriving in about twenty minutes.

2. When Michiko lit a cigarette in the restaurant and began smoking, the waiter gave her a _____approving look.

3. The smell of fish is awful in here! Is there anything we can do to _____odorize this room?

4. When we get off the plane we have to _____embark through the door on the left.

5. At the end of the concert, the crowd began to _____perse and within twenty minutes, almost everyone had left the building.

C Can you think of an antonym for each of the new words you've learned in this exercise? Share your ideas with a partner.

Think About It   **Discuss the following questions with a partner.**

1. *Do you think the research that astronauts and agencies like NASA are doing is important? Explain your answer.*

2. *Do you think that there is intelligent life elsewhere in the universe? Do you think that perhaps extraterrestrials have visited our planet? Explain your answer.*

3. *Given the serious physiological and psychological difficulties that astronauts face, do you think we should send humans on long space missions, or would it be better to use robots?*

4. *What difficulties might an astronaut on a three-year trip to Mars face? Make a list and think of a possible solution for each difficulty. Share your ideas with your classmates.*

Discuss the following questions with a partner.

1. Look at the photo above. In 2001, this man made history. What do you think he did?

2. Look at the title of the reading passage. What things might a person on a 'space vacation' do and see?

3. What kind of person do you think would want to be a 'space tourist'?

4. The following words and phrases are all in the reading:

milestone   once-in-a-lifetime   stand in the way   civilian   pave the way

What does each word or phrase mean? How does each relate to the topic of the reading?

Time yourself as you read through the passage. Try to read as fluently as you can. Record your time in the Reading Rate Chart on page 202.

A Space Vacation _____

In 1969, a key milestone in space travel was reached when Neil Armstrong set foot on the moon. In 2001, another landmark event took place when the first civilian traveled into space as a paying tourist.

As a teenager, Dennis Tito dreamed of visiting outer space. As a young man, he aspired to become an astronaut and earned a bachelor's and a master's degree in aerospace engineering. However, Tito did not have all the qualities necessary to become a professional astronaut, so instead, he went to work as a space engineer in one of NASA's

5

Your reading rate may change slightly, depending on the type of material you are reading. Don't let this discourage you; your goal should always be smooth, fluent reading.

laboratories for five years. Later, Tito set up his own financial
10 investment company and, eventually, he became a multi-millionaire.
Later in life, the ex-rocket engineer, still passionate about space travel,
began looking into ways to make a trip into space.

In the early 1990s, the Soviet Space Agency was offering tickets for a
visit to the Mir space station to anyone who could afford it. Tito
15 jumped at the chance[1] for this once-in-a-lifetime experience. Due to
political and economic changes in the former Soviet Union, however,
Tito's trip was postponed and later, Mir was decommissioned.[2] In 2001,
Tito's dream finally came true when he paid a rumored $20 million and
took off aboard a SOYUZ rocket to deliver supplies to the
20 International Space Station, a joint venture[3] between the space agencies
of Japan, Canada, Europe, Russia, and the U.S.

In preparation for the trip, Tito trained at the Gagarin Cosmonauts
Training Center at Star City in Russia. There, he underwent eight
months of physical fitness training, weightless simulations, and a
25 variety of other exercises to prepare him for space travel. Although the
Russians believed that Tito was adequately prepared for the trip, NASA
thought otherwise. Dennis Tito had to sign an agreement with
international space officials taking financial responsibility for any
equipment he damaged or broke on his trip. He was also barred from
30 entering any part of the space station owned by the U.S. unless
escorted.

Although Tito made history and paved the way for the future of space
tourism, factors such as cost, and the amount of training required,
stand in the way of space vacations becoming an option for most
35 people in the near future. In spite of this, Japanese and North American
market research data shows that there is definite public interest in space
travel. In a 1993 survey of 3,030 Japanese, 80 percent of those under
the age of forty said they would like to visit space at least once. Seventy
percent of this group would pay up to three month's salary for the trip.
40 In 1995, 1,020 households in North America were surveyed and of
those, 60 percent were interested in a vacation in space. Seventy-five
percent of those interested were under forty years of age. Just over 45
percent said they would pay three month's salary, around 18 percent
said they would pay six month's salary, and nearly 11 percent would
45 pay a year's salary. Two-thirds of those who want to visit space would
like to do so several times.

Although these statistics have now become out-of-date, the reactions
from America, Canada, and Japan alone indicate that space travel is a

potential multi-billion dollar business. However, since the nature of this type of travel makes it hazardous to humans, it would have to be restricted to those who are physically fit and able to take responsibility for the risks involved. As in the early days of commercial aviation,[4] space travel will initially be an option only for the wealthy. In the future, however, reasonably priced trips may offer many the chance of a vacation in space.

50

55

---

[1] **jump at the chance** to eagerly and quickly do or take something that is offered
[2] **decommission** to stop using something, usually weapons or large equipment
[3] **joint venture** a business partnership between two or more people or organizations
[4] **aviation** related to air travel and the design and production of aircraft

---

Reading Comprehension: How Much Do You Remember?

(A) Choose the best answer for each question or statement below. Try not to look back at the reading for the answers.

1. Dennis Tito made the first trip as a space tourist _____.
   a. in the late '60s   **b.** in the early '90s   **c.** this century

2. Which of the following is NOT true about Dennis Tito?
   a. He has an advanced degree in aerospace engineering.
   b. He is now an astronaut for NASA.
   c. He eventually became a very wealthy man.

3. Tito's first trip into space was with _____ to _____.
   a. the Russians / the International Space Station
   b. the Americans / SOYUZ
   c. members of the former Soviet Union / the Mir space station

4. Which of the following describes NASA's feelings about Tito's trip into space?
   a. extremely proud   **b.** somewhat eager   **c.** very concerned

5. According to a Japanese survey, which of the following is true?
   a. Eighty percent of all those interviewed would be interested in traveling to space.
   b. Some people would pay a quarter of their annual salary to visit space.
   c. Only people under the age of forty are interested in space travel.

6. According to a North American survey on space travel, which is true?
   a. Seventy-five percent of those surveyed would be interested in traveling to space.
   b. Most people would pay a year's salary to visit space as a tourist.
   c. Most of the people interested in space travel were under the age of forty.

7. Which of the following would probably prevent you from becoming a space tourist in the near future?
   a. health   **b.** wealth   **c.** youth

(B) Check your answers with a partner. Count how many you got correct—be honest! Then, fill in the Reading Comprehension Chart on page 202.

Vocabulary Comprehension:
Odd Word Out

Ⓐ For each group, circle the word that does not belong. The words in *italics* are vocabulary items from the reading.

1. *milestone*	failure	goal	event
2. general	soldier	sergeant	*civilian*
3. indifferent about	*aspire (to)*	hope for	want to
4. special	average	*once-in-a-lifetime*	unique
5. invite	*bar*	exclude	prohibit
6. unattended	unaccompanied	solitary	*escorted*
7. make possible	enable	*stand in the way*	*pave the way*
8. *out-of-date*	modern	current	up-to-date

Ⓑ Complete the sentences using the words in *italics* from A. Be sure to use the correct form of the word.

1. All _____ are required to wear a guest pass in order to visit the army base.

2. Graduating from university is an important _____ in one's life.

3. I thought Naomi was coming to the concert alone but she arrived _____ by Ben.

4. Since his fight with the waiter, Roberto has been _____ from the restaurant.

5. Young-hee originally _____ to become a physician, but in the end she became a dentist.

6. If your family is willing to pay for you to live for a year in London, you should go! It's a _____ opportunity you may not get again.

7. I bought this software for my computer less than a year ago, but it's already _____.

8. Claudia gets good grades and did well on her entrance exam. What could possibly _____ of her getting into a good university?

9. Mathematicians like Newton and Kepler _____ for the future of space travel with their ideas about how objects might move in space.

Ⓐ Look at how compound adjectives are formed.

1. Some compound adjectives are formed by joining two words to form another word.

*an **outspoken** man*   *a **secondhand** car*

2. Other compound adjectives can be formed by combining two or more words using hyphens.

*Is Yuri Gagarin well known in your country?   Is he a **well-known** astronaut?*

*Karina's daughter is five years old.   Karina has a **five-year-old** daughter.*

3. Some compound adjectives are fixed—the word order is always the same and they are always hyphenated.

*He's an **easy-going** guy.   These statistics are **out-of-date**.*

> *In this chapter, you learned the compound adjectives 'once-in-a-lifetime' and 'out-of-date.' Compound adjectives are formed when two or more nouns, adjectives, adverbs, or the participle form of a verb (e.g., 'dressed,' 'looking') are combined to modify a noun.*

Ⓑ What do you think the following compound adjectives mean? Complete the sentences with the correct adjective, then write a simple definition for each.

> **up-to-the-minute**   **over-the-counter**
> **out-of-the-way**   **matter-of-fact**   **middle-aged**

1. In order to have some privacy, Erik and Laura stayed at a(n) _____ villa in the Colorado mountains.
Definition: _____

2. If you want _____ information on the election results, tune in to channel 4.
Definition: _____

3. I don't know exactly what the robber looked like; he had grayish hair and appeared to be _____.
Definition: _____

4. In the U.S., you can't buy medicine such as antibiotics _____. You can only get them with a prescription.
Definition: _____

5. Antonio talked about failing his test in a very _____ way; it didn't seem to bother him at all.
Definition: _____

Ⓒ Now write three sentences using any of the compound adjectives you have learned. Share your ideas with a partner.

1. _____

2. _____

3. _____

What Do You Think?

Discuss the following questions with a partner.

1. *Would you be interested in traveling to space as a tourist? Why or why not? How much would you pay for a space vacation?*
2. *What do you think of NASA's treatment of Dennis Tito? Do you think the agency was right to limit his actions during his visit to the space station?*
3. *Do you think that space tourism will be possible for the average person in your lifetime? Why?*
4. *Talk about something you aspire to do. Is there anything that is standing in the way of you achieving your goal?*

Real Life Skill

Understanding Travel Vocabulary

Many travel brochures and websites provide information in English on holiday trips and hotels. Understanding the most common words and phrases can help you make the best possible travel choices.

Ⓐ Look at the underlined words in the first hotel brochure below. Match each with a definition.

1. free, no charge: _____
2. an extra cost: _____
3. the rooms in a hotel: _____
4. places or services that are useful and enable people to do things:

   _____
5. things that make life comfortable or convenient: _____

Ⓑ In the first hotel brochure, under which section would you list the following items?

> phone with voice mail   dry cleaner   suite   Internet cafe

1. **The Somerset Hotel**

   Phone: (212) 555-9987

   Accommodation*: 200 rooms

   Single rooms: from $65 a night
   Doubles: from $100 a night

   Room amenities:
   satellite TV, minibar, hair dryer

   Complimentary breakfast served daily from 6:00–10:00 a.m

   Facilities:
   Health club, two restaurants, gift shop, business center, rooftop swimming pool

   *a surcharge of 5% will be added to rooms of over $200 a night

2. **Collingsworth Inn**

   Phone: (212) 555-4456

   Accommodation*: 50 rooms

   Single rooms: from $100 a night
   Doubles: from $175 a night

   Room amenities:
   TV, kitchen, hair dryer

   Complimentary breakfast served daily from 6:00–10:00 a.m

   Facilities:
   swimming pool

   *a surcharge of 8% will be added to rooms of over $200 a night

Ⓒ You and a friend are planning to visit the National Air and Space Museum at the Smithsonian Institution in Washington, D.C. Which hotel will you stay at? Explain your reasons to a partner.

The Changing Family

Getting Ready

Discuss the following questions with a partner.

1. *Describe the family in the photo above. How do you think the members are related? Are families like this common in your country?*

2. *How do you think the family has changed over the last twenty or thirty years? Explain your answer.*

3. *Do you think that changes to the family over the last twenty or thirty years have been positive or negative? Explain your answer.*

4. *How do you think the family unit will change in the future?*

Before You Read:
Having Children

(A) Look at the statements below. Write F next to the statements that express facts. Write O next to the opinions. Underline the words that helped you decide which is a fact and which is an opinion.

1. A mother's role is more important than a father's. _____

2. Today, many parents are choosing to have only one or two children. _____

3. Having more than one child might be better for both family and society. _____

4. The cost of raising a child in the U.S. is now about $18,000 a year. _____

5. Some parents are choosing to have fewer children probably because it's too expensive. _____

(B) The following words and phrases can all be found in the reading. What does each mean? How is each related to topic of the reading?

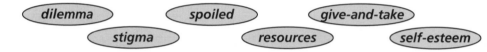

dilemma   spoiled   give-and-take

stigma   resources   self-esteem

Reading Skill:
Identifying Fact versus Opinion

A fact is something that can be checked and proven. An opinion is one's personal belief or feeling about something. Opinions often include words and phrases like 'in my opinion,' 'believe,' 'think,' 'might,' 'may,' 'probably,' 'should.' A lot of what we read can be a mixture of fact and opinion. Being able to tell the difference between the two can help you to understand a reading better, and to make choices about what to do with the information.

(A) Read the passage below and in each paragraph, underline the sentences that express facts. Circle the sentences that express opinion.

Is an Only Child a Lonely Child? _____

This month in *Family Planning* magazine, child psychologist Dr. Ethan Wood answers a question from Andrea Gonzales who writes:

Q: Dear Dr. Wood,
My husband and I are facing a dilemma, namely the issue of whether to
5 have a second child—we already have one healthy, happy five-year-old daughter. Both of us have demanding jobs, and limited time and financial resources, but we're also very keen to ensure[1] that our only child does not become a lonely child. So, what are the pros and cons of having a second child?

10 **A: Dear Andrea,**
This is one of the most difficult issues that parents nowadays face. As you point out, a concern that is often heard with regard to single children is whether one child necessarily means a lonely child. Many single-child parents feel a stigma associated with their decision to have
15 only one child. There are no other children in the family for the child to

associate with, and this may lead to the child feeling lonely at times, especially during vacations.

Another common argument against having just one child is that an only child may be more spoiled than one with siblings.[2] Many people believe that a single child will not have learned to negotiate with others, and respect the give-and-take involved in many relationships. Some think this may leave the child less capable of interacting well with people his or her own age than one who has been raised with siblings.

Despite these arguments, the number of parents choosing to have only one child is increasing in many parts of the world. In the U.S., for example, 14 percent of women between 18 and 34 plan to have just one child, and this percentage is expected to rise. The same trend can be seen in the U.K. According to the Family Policy Studies Center, the overall number of British children being born each year has declined. In Japan, the average number of children born per family had declined to 1.42 by 1996, while latest statistics cite less than one child. This has led to government concerns about supporting an increasing population of elderly people in the future; it is predicted that, by 2020, a third of the population in Japan will be aged 65 or over.

For some single-child parents, particularly those with busy careers, the pressures of devoting time and energy to a second child can seem too overwhelming, resulting in them electing[3] to have no more children. For other parents, the financial burden of having a second child may be the prime consideration. According to government surveys, many couples in Japan choose not to have large families as the cost of supporting a child up to the age of 18 is estimated to be around 20 million yen, equivalent to around US$160,000.

Advocates of single-child families argue that there are advantages for the child as well as the parents. With just one child, they suggest, there is less potential for family arguments arising from favoritism or sibling jealousy. Moreover, with only one child, the parents can give, and the child can receive, more quality time and attention. This often leads to increased self-esteem which, combined with increased independence, can lead to the child being more confident.

Unfortunately, Andrea, there is no simple answer to the question of whether or not to have a second child. The circumstances affecting each set of parents are unique, and what is appropriate for one family may not be for another. The important thing, in the end, is to make a decision that both you and your husband feel confident about.

¹ **ensure** to make sure
² **siblings** brothers or sisters
³ **electing** choosing to do something

Ⓑ Write F next to the statements that express facts from the reading. Write O next to the statements that express opinions.

1. Andrea Gonzales and her husband have a five-year-old child. _____

2. Andrea and her husband might not have enough time and money for a second child. _____

3. Many parents with only one child face a certain amount of social pressure to have more. _____

4. An only child might feel lonelier than a child with siblings. _____

5. Only children tend to be more spoiled than those with siblings. _____

6. Many married couples in Japan are choosing to have no children or only one child _____

7. Some people choose not to have two children because they are too busy. Others choose not to because they can't afford it. _____

8. In families with only one child, there tends to be less arguing and sibling competition. _____

9. Only children tend to be more self-confident and independent. _____

Reading Comprehension:
What Do You Remember?

Decide if the following statements about the reading are true (*T*) or false (*F*). If you check (✔) false, correct the statement to make it true.

	T	F
1. Andrea Gonzales's husband works; she is a housewife.		
2. According to Dr. Wood, an only child might feel most lonely during vacation periods.		
3. Some people believe that only children are spoiled because they don't receive enough attention from adults.		
4. In the U.S., women between 18 and 34 are planning to have more than one child in the future.		
5. The Japanese government fears that the elderly won't have people to care for them in the future.		
6. Today, the cost of raising one child to age 18 exceeds US$100,000.		
7. Dr. Wood suggests that Andrea Gonzales and her husband should probably not have another child.		

Ⓐ For each group, circle the word that does not belong. The words in *italics* are vocabulary items from the reading.

1. *demanding*	difficult	effortless	challenging
2. compromise	insist	cooperate	*negotiate*
3. solution	*dilemma*	problem	difficult choice
4. shame	pride	*stigma*	disgrace
5. pampered	*spoiled*	overindulged	thoughtful
6. supply	debt	savings	*resources*
7. cooperation	demand	*give-and-take*	negotiation
8. *self-esteem*	self-confidence	self-worth	selfishness
9. first	*prime*	secondary	main

Ⓑ Complete the e-mail below using the words in *italics* from A. Be sure to use the correct form of the word.

Dear Dr. Wood,

I read with interest your reply to Andrea Gonzales about whether or not she and her husband should have another child. I, too, am facing a similar (1)_____ related to having children; my fiancé wants us to start a family after we are married, but I don't. I do realize that marriage is all about (2)_____, but this is one thing I am not willing to (3)_____. I don't want to be a mother. It's not because I am a selfish person, or was a (4)_____ child myself; I come from a very large and loving family, and I get along wonderfully with both my parents and siblings. My (5)_____ reason for not wanting to be a parent is because I am a twenty-eight-year-old woman who has a (6)_____ job as an artist—which I love. I would prefer to put all of my emotional and financial (7)_____ into developing my career rather than having children. Unfortunately, my fiancé does not feel the same way, nor, to my surprise do many of my female friends. You can't imagine the (8)_____ attached to being a woman who says she doesn't want children. Honestly, some people look at me like I'm a monster! Though I have strong feelings about this, I must admit my (9)_____ has suffered terribly in the past few months; I sometimes wonder if I am making the right decision. If I choose not to have children, I know, too, that my fiancé will probably not want to get married. What should I do?

Mariah
Miami, Florida

Vocabulary Skill:

Compound Nouns

In this chapter, you learned the compound nouns 'give-and-take' and 'self-esteem.' Compound nouns are two or more nouns, adjectives, adverbs, or verbs that work together to talk about one person, place, or thing.

(A) Look at how compound nouns are formed. What parts of speech are joined together to form each?

1. Some compound nouns join two words together to form one word.

   A low **birthrate**   children's **software**   Let's eat **takeout**.

2. Some compound nouns are two words that work together to refer to one thing.

   family planning   **maternity leave**   **family tree**

3. Some compound nouns are formed by joining two or more words together with hyphens.

   High **self-esteem**   A lot of **give-and-take**   John's **mother-in-law**

(B) Join one word from the box with a word below to form a compound noun. Is each compound written as one word, two words, or is it hyphenated? Use your dictionary to help you.

in-law	sitter	mother	license
friend	style	control	wife

1. father _____
2. boy _____
3. self _____
4. baby _____
5. driver's _____
6. house _____
7. grand _____
8. life _____

(C) Match each compound noun with the correct definition below.

1. a person who takes care of children while the parents are out

   _____

2. a woman who stays home and takes care of the house and children

   _____

3. one's male companion or lover _____
4. the male parent of one's spouse _____
5. your father or mother's mother _____
6. one's chosen way of living _____
7. legal permission to use a car _____
8. the ability to remain calm and not show one's feelings; will power

   _____

Think About It   Discuss the following questions with a partner.

1. *Do you think that only children tend to be lonely or more spoiled than those with siblings? Explain your answer.*
2. *How many people are there in your family? If you have siblings, do you get along with them? Would you prefer to be an only child? If you are an only child, do you wish you had siblings?*

Discuss the following questions with a partner.

1. Quickly write down five words that relate to the word *mother*. Do the same for the word *father*. Compare your word lists. How are they similar or different?

2. When you were a child, who looked after, or took care of, you? How often did you spend time with your father? What sort of things did you do together?

3. How is being a father today different from fatherhood twenty or thirty years ago?

4. The following words and phrases can all be found in the reading. What does each mean? How do you think each is related to the topic of the reading?

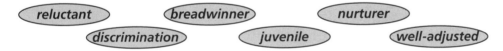

reluctant   breadwinner   nurturer   discrimination   juvenile   well-adjusted

Reading Skill:
Developing Reading Fluency

Time yourself as you read through the passage. Try to read as fluently as you can. Record your time in the Reading Rate Chart on page 202.

Changing Roles: Stay-at-Home Dads _____

> *Developing reading fluency means improving your reading speed and your comprehension rate at the same time.*

British mechanic Neil Walkingshaw was looking for a way to care for his newborn child when he approached his boss with a proposal[1] in early 2000. Reluctant to hire a babysitter once his wife's maternity leave[2] ended and she returned to work, Walkingshaw asked if he could switch to part-time hours in order to spend half of each day at home looking after his son. His employer refused, saying the paperwork would be "too messy" and that it would be difficult to get anyone to share Walkingshaw's job. Knowing that the company he worked for had granted similar requests to female employees, Walkingshaw sued[3] on the grounds of sex discrimination. On November 20, 2001, an industrial tribunal[4] ruled that Walkingshaw had been discriminated

5

10

against and awarded him £3,600. The ruling is believed to be the first of its kind, and demonstrates just how much views on parental roles have changed over the years.

15　As little as thirty years ago, few people questioned the gender roles that had prevailed for centuries. The conventional wisdom[5] was that a woman's place was in the home and that a man's main responsibility to his family was to put food on the table. In the 1970s and '80s, however, greater numbers of working women meant that men were no longer the
20　sole[6] breadwinner. A father's emotional involvement with his family also became more important. Forty years ago, almost no husbands were present in the delivery room when their wives gave birth. Today, it is generally expected for male partners to attend childbirth classes, be there for the delivery, and to take more responsibility for child rearing[7]
25　than their fathers or grandfathers did.

In addition to society's changing views of the role men play in relation to childcare, social scientists are also re-examining the contribution a father makes to his child's welfare and development. Researchers have found evidence to suggest that a father plays a role in child
30　development that is quite different from that of the mother. According to the research, fathers tend to be more playful, thus encouraging children to develop in a different way emotionally and physically than a child might under a mother's exclusive care.

Studies have also found that the presence of the father in the home can
35　contribute to lower juvenile crime rates, a decrease in child poverty, and lower rates of teenage pregnancy. Differences in parenting styles between men and women are also believed to contribute to children's ability to understand and communicate emotions in different ways. The research supports claims by some groups that the absence of a father in
40　the family is the single biggest social problem in modern society.

In recent years, organizations like the U.S.-based National Fatherhood Initiative have begun to argue that the presence of the father is vital to a child's development. These organizations aim to encourage fathers to take a more active role in their children's lives. The movement also calls
45　for the creation of a new image of fatherhood, one that goes beyond the traditional view of the father solely as provider, and also includes the equally crucial roles of nurturer, moral example, disciplinarian and teacher.

Many family experts believe that the ability of a family to raise well-
50　adjusted children has much to do with a society promoting healthy

families. If this theory is true, and if the father's role is as important as the mother's in raising children, it's possible to imagine a day when society will value the role of the father more, and when all men will learn to take their paternal duties as seriously as Neil Walkingshaw.

---

¹ **proposal** a suggestion or an offer
² **maternity leave** period of time after a woman has a child, usually 3–6 months, when she takes time off from work
³ **sue** to file a lawsuit against someone to protect one's legal rights
⁴ **tribunal** a court of law
⁵ **conventional wisdom** traditional or usual view or opinion
⁶ **sole** only
⁷ **rearing** caring and education of the young in order for them to grow

---

Reading Comprehension: What Do You Remember?

Ⓐ How much do you remember from the reading? Choose the best answer for each question below. Try not to look back at the reading for the answers.

1. In early 2000, Neil Walkingshaw _____.
   a. was looking for a babysitter to take care of his child.
   b. wanted to work fewer hours so that he could care for his child.
   c. tried to convince his wife to stay home and care for their child.

2. Which of the following is NOT true about Walkingshaw's story?
   a. He sued his employer for unfair treatment.   **b.** He had to pay a £3,600 fine.
   c. His employer allowed new mothers to work part-time.

3. By the 1980s, more women were _____, and fewer men were _____.
   a. in the workplace / the main source of income
   b. having children / in the delivery room   **c.** getting jobs / in the workplace

4. According to the reading, fathers today are expected to _____ than they did 30–40 years ago.
   a. earn more money   **b.** take more responsibility for child rearing
   c. have children later

5. Research now suggests that _____.
   a. fathers contribute in unique ways to the development of children
   b. households without fathers don't risk any serious social problems
   c. fathers tend to be more demanding with their children than mothers

6. Some people would like to see the image of fatherhood include the role of _____ in addition to provider.
   a. breadwinner   **b.** friend   **c.** caretaker

7. According to the final paragraph, society now _____.
   a. sees the role of father and mother as equal
   b. needs to do more to help fathers become involved parents
   c. is doing all it can to help parents raise happy, healthy children

Vocabulary Comprehension:
Words in Context

(B) Check your answers with a partner. Count how many you got correct—be honest! Then, fill in the Reading Comprehension Chart on page 202.

(A) The words in *italics* are vocabulary items from the reading. Read each question or statement and choose the correct answer. Compare your answers with a partner.

1. Which might a person be *reluctant* to do?
   a. write a term paper   **b.** send a friend an e-mail

2. A person _____ 18 is considered a *juvenile* in many countries.
   a. over   **b.** under

3. Which occupation might require a person to be more of a *nurturer*?
   a. police officer   **b.** doctor

4. The *breadwinner* typically _____ money.
   a. earns   **b.** spends

5. Which is *crucial* for a child to receive in the first few years of its life?
   a. music   **b.** attention

6. Which would be an example of *discrimination*?
   a. paying someone less money because of his or her age
   b. allowing parents to leave work early when a child is sick

7. If someone is concerned about your *welfare*, he or she is primarily interested in your _____.
   a. level of intelligence   **b.** health and happiness

8. During the Middle Ages, which common belief *prevailed*?
   a. the Earth was flat   **b.** there was life on other planets

9. A *well-adjusted* person is typically not _____.
   a. violent   **b.** stable

(B) Now think of other examples using the vocabulary from A. Discuss your ideas with a partner.

1. Name something else a person might be *reluctant* to do?
2. When is a person no longer considered a *juvenile* in your country?
3. Name another occupation that might require a person to be more of a *nurturer*.
4. Who is the *breadwinner* in your family?
5. Name something else that is *crucial* for a child to receive in the first few years of its life?
6. Give another example of *discrimination*. Is this form of discrimination common in your country?
7. Are you responsible for anyone's *welfare*? How do you take care of this person?
8. Talk about a social or scientific belief that *prevails* today. Do you agree with it?
9. Do you think that you are a *well-adjusted* person?

Vocabulary Skill:
Root Words
pater, mater,
and *juv*

(A) Study the words in the chart. What do you think they mean? Match a word with a definition below. Use your dictionary to help you.

Noun	Verb	Adjective
matriarch	to mother	maternal
maternity		
patriarch	patronize	patriotic
paternity	to father	paternal
juvenile	rejuvenate	juvenile

In this chapter, you read the adjectives 'juvenile' and 'paternal.' There are many words in English that begin with or include the root words 'juv' meaning 'young,' 'pater/patri' meaning 'father,' and 'mater/matri' meaning 'mother.'

1. to talk down to someone, to speak to a person like a child _____
2. the female leader of a family, usually the oldest or wisest _____
3. related to motherhood or pregnancy _____
4. loyal to a country _____
5. to care for or nurture someone _____
6. to feel refreshed again, usually after a rest _____
7. related to fatherhood or being a father _____
8. young; can also mean childish or immature _____
9. the male leader of a family, usually the oldest or wisest _____
10. related to the mother _____

(B) Read each question below. Then, take turns asking and answering the questions with a partner.

1. What is the name of your maternal grandmother?
2. How old is your paternal grandfather?
3. Give an example of juvenile behavior.
4. Is maternity leave common in your country? How much time off work do women usually take?
5. Talk about something that rejuvenates you.
6. Are you a patriotic person?
7. Is there a patriarch or matriarch in your family? Describe this person.

What Do You Think?

Discuss the following questions with a partner.

1. *Do you think that men face any sort of social discrimination? Give an example.*
2. *In your country, do you think that men participate equally in child rearing? Explain your answer.*
3. *In some countries, stay-at-home dads are becoming more common. What do you think of this? Is this trend happening in your country?*

Real Life Skill

Family Members

In this unit, you've read about the changing family. In today's world, many people's families include more than their biological parents and siblings. There are some common names used to refer to these types of relatives.

Ⓐ Look at the words and phrases below. Match each with a definition.

1. mother-in-law _____
2. ex-wife _____
3. step-brother _____
4. half brother _____
5. to adopt _____
6. step-mother _____

a. to legally make another person's child a member of your family

b. a brother related to you by marriage only

c. your father's wife; your mother by marriage only

d. your spouse's mother

e. your former spouse

f. a brother who shares the same mother or father as you

Ⓑ Read the newspaper announcement below. Then, using the words and phrases from A, answer the questions that follow. Be sure to use the correct form of the word or phrase.

Hollywood Couple Announces New Family Addition

Hollywood — Spokesperson for actor Nicole Sommers announced yesterday that Ms. Sommers is expecting a baby girl with husband Miguel Santiago in May. It is the couple's first child. Ms. Sommers has a daughter from a previous marriage, Michelle, aged 7, now living with her father, director Cameron DuBois. Mr. Santiago has twin boys, Alberto and Jorge, age 10, who live with his ex-wife. The news of the new baby comes just three months after Sommers and Santiago adopted a little girl whom they've named Angelina. Ms. Sommers is currently shooting her latest film in the south of Spain, where she is staying with her in-laws. She has not announced plans to stop working at this time.

1. Miguel Santiago is Michelle's _____.
2. Alberto and Jorge are Michelle's _____.
3. The new baby will be Jorge and Alberto's _____.
4. Ms. Sommer's in-laws are Miguel Santiago's _____.
5. Alberto and Jorge are Nicole Sommers's _____.
6. Cameron DuBois is Ms. Sommers's _____.
7. Angelina is Michelle, Alberto, and Jorge's _____.

Education

Getting Ready

Discuss the following questions with a partner.

1. *Look at the photos above. How do the two situations differ?*
2. *Are there different types of schools and colleges in your country? What are they and how are they different?*
3. *Do you think the educational system in your country is effective? Why?*
4. *Do you think parents should be able to choose how their children are educated, or should it be the government's responsibility? Why?*

Before You Read:
Going to School

Discuss the following questions with a partner.

1. Did you enjoy attending school when you were younger? Why?

2. What do you understand by the term *homeschooling*?

3. What do you think the benefits of homeschooling are? What are the drawbacks? Make a list for each. Which list is longer?

4. The following words and phrases can all be found in the reading. What does each mean? How is each related to the topic of the reading?

escalating   establish   peers   secure   competent   alternative

Reading Skill:
Arguing For and Against a Topic

Many reading passages present two sides of an argument—one argues for, or in favor of, the topic; the other argues against it. Phrases such as 'advocates of' and 'in favor of' signal that information that supports the topic will be introduced. Phrases like 'critics of' or 'concerns about' signal that information against the topic is coming. Also, words and phrases like 'but,' 'however,' 'though,' 'in contrast,' and 'in spite of' signal that an opposite or different opinion is about to be introduced.

Ⓐ Read the passage below and complete the chart with information from the reading.

HOMESCHOOLING	
Reasons For	**Reasons Against**
1. _____	1. _____
2. _____	2. _____
3. _____	3. _____
4. _____	
5. _____	
6. _____	
7. _____	

Homeschooling—a Better Way to Learn?

Increasing numbers of parents in the U.S. are choosing to teach their kids at home. In fact, the U.S. Department of Education estimated that, in 1999, around 850,000 children were being homeschooled. Some educational experts say the real figure is about double this estimate,
5 and the ranks[1] of homeschooled children appear to be growing at a rate of about 11 percent annually.

At one time, there was a stigma associated with homeschooling; it was traditionally used for students who could not attend school because of behavioral or learning difficulties. Today, however, more parents are
10 taking on the responsibility of educating their children at home due to dissatisfaction with the educational system. Many parents are unhappy about class size, as well as problems inside the classroom. Teacher

shortages and lack of funding mean that, in many schools, one teacher is responsible for thirty or forty pupils. The result is often that children are deprived of the attention they need. Escalating classroom violence has also motivated some parents to remove their children from school.

Advocates[2] of homeschooling believe that children learn better when they are in a secure, loving environment. Many psychologists see the home as the most natural learning environment, and originally the home was the classroom, long before schools were established. Parents who homeschool argue that they can monitor their children's education and give them the attention that is lacking in a traditional school setting. Students can also pick and choose what to study and when to study, thus enabling them to learn at their own pace.

In contrast, critics[3] of homeschooling say that children who are not in the classroom miss out on learning important social skills because they have little interaction with their peers. Several studies, though, have shown that the home-educated appear to do just as well in terms of social and emotional development as other students, having spent more time in the comfort and security of their home, with guidance from parents who care about their welfare. In spite of this, many critics of homeschooling have raised concerns about the ability of parents to teach their kids effectively. Many parents who homeschool have no teacher training and are not competent educators of all the subjects taught in schools. In terms of academic achievement, however, homeschooled children do just as well as those who have been in the classroom, and many walk the campuses of Harvard and Stanford alongside the conventionally educated.

With an increasing number of disgruntled parents taking their children out of class, schools are receiving less money in per-pupil funding. Some see this as a threat to the system, and argue that schools will never be able to improve their situation and restore[4] parents' confidence in the educational system. Many schools have opened their doors to homeschoolers on a part-time basis, allowing these children to attend classes once or twice a week, or take part in extracurricular activities[5] such as playing football or taking ballet lessons. While parents will not

completely put their confidence back into the system, many of them
55 have reached a compromise that allows their children the extra benefits
of peer interaction and access to a wider choice of activities.

Whatever the arguments for or against it, homeschooling in the U.S.
has become a multi-million dollar industry, and it is growing. There are
now websites, support groups, and conventions[6] that help parents to
60 assert their rights and enable them to learn more about educating their
children. Though once the last resort[7] for troubled children,
homeschooling today is an accepted alternative to an educational
system that some believe is failing.

---

[1] **the ranks** the numbers
[2] **advocate** a person who believes in something and strongly supports and promotes it
[3] **critic** a person who disapproves of or dislikes something
[4] **restore** to return something to the way it once was
[5] **extracurricular activities** extra activities done after class, usually for fun, but also for study
[6] **conventions** large meetings of people who share the same interests or occupation, usually held once a year
[7] **the last resort** the only choice remaining because everything else has failed

---

B Now read the passage again, then answer the questions that follow.

Reading Comprehension: What Do You Remember?

How much do you remember from the reading? Complete the sentences with the correct answer, then share your answers with a partner.

1. In 1999, _____ children in the United States were homeschooled, but that number is probably closer to _____.

2. At one time, homeschooling was a method of education confined to the ranks of students with _____.

3. Now many parents homeschool as they are unhappy about classroom _____ and the increase in classroom _____.

4. Before schools were created, many people learned _____.

5. Homeschooled children are now attending universities such as _____.

6. Some homeschooled children are returning to traditional schools part-time in order to take part in _____.

7. Parents who choose to homeschool their children can learn to teach them through

_____

Vocabulary Comprehension: Word Definitions

Ⓐ Look at the list of words and phrases from the reading. Match each with a definition on the right.

1. escalating _____

2. secure _____

3. motivated _____

4. miss out on _____

5. peer _____

6. alternative _____

7. disgruntled _____

8. competent _____

9. take on _____

a. a person of one's own age

b. capable, knowledgeable, or experienced

c. increasing, usually in a negative or dangerous way

d. to accept or agree to do something

e. safe and protected

f. unhappy or displeased with something, often used to describe a person

g. to lose or not have a chance to do something that is fun or interesting

h. driven by a strong desire to do something

i. another option or choice, usually one that is different from the norm

Ⓑ Complete the sentences below using the vocabulary from A. Be sure to use the correct form of the word.

1. Kotaro is just too busy to _____ any more work. Ask Sandy to take notes at the meeting.

2. A lot of people are exploring Eastern medicine as an _____ to Western medical treatment.

3. Ji-young is very _____ to succeed in business so she works long hours every day.

4. Experts are worried that _____ inflation may cause prices of food and gas to increase again this month.

5. Do you really feel _____ living alone in a dangerous part of the city?

6. Jamie is quite _____ in corresponding with our Japanese clients as he lived in Japan for ten years.

7. We didn't arrive until 9:00 and _____ Gina's wonderful dinner.

8. Mei was _____ about not receiving an A on her term paper.

9. Are most of your _____ still living at home with their parents, or do they have their own apartments?

Vocabulary Skill:

The Root Word *ven/ vent*

In this chapter, you read the adjective 'conventional,' meaning 'usual' or 'traditional,' and the noun form 'convention' meaning 'a large meeting of people.' Both words include the root word 'ven,' meaning 'to come.' 'Ven,' sometimes also written as 'vent,' is combined with prefixes and suffixes to form many words in English.

Ⓐ For each word, study the different parts. Then, write its part of speech and a simple definition. Use your dictionary to help you. Share your ideas with a partner.

Vocabulary	Part of Speech	Definition
1. conventional	_adjective_	_usual or traditional_
2. convene		
3. circumvent		
4. intervene		
5. inventory		
6. revenue		
7. prevention		

Ⓑ Complete each sentence using the words from the chart. Be sure to use the correct form of the word.

1. The key to staying healthy is _____—don't smoke, drink too much, and try to visit your doctor once a year for a full health check.

2. A large crowd _____ in front of the university to hear the president speak.

3. Before Carl could hit Scott, Brett _____ and stopped the fight.

4. Thanks to a great sales team, the company has almost doubled its _____ this year.

5. In the U.S., cigarette companies can't advertise on TV. However, many of these companies _____ this rule by advertising at sporting events that are televised.

6. I'm afraid we don't have any more of Yo-Yo Ma's CDs in our _____, but I can order a copy of his latest release if you like.

Ⓒ Can you think of any other words in English that include the root *ven/vent*?

Think About It	Discuss the following questions with a partner.

1. *In schools in your country, do you think teachers give students enough attention in class?*

2. *Up to this point in your life, do you think you've received a good education or not? Why?*

3. *Are you in favor of, or against, homeschooling? Why?*

4. *At school, do you now, or did you in the past, participate in any extracurricular activities? Which ones? Did you enjoy them?*

Discuss the following questions with a partner.

1. What do you know about the history of education in your country? How do you think education has changed over the last 100 years?

2. How old is your school or university? Do you know by whom, and when, it was founded?

3. Describe the teachers you had in high school. How did they treat students? Who was your favorite teacher?

4. The following words can all be found in the reading. What does each mean? How do you think each is related to the topic of the reading?

formal   reform   harsh   compulsory   haphazard

Time yourself as you read through the passage. Try to read as fluently as you can. Record your time in the Reading Rate Chart on page 202.

The History of School _____

In modern developed societies, access to formal education is something that many people now take for granted. Formal schools have not always existed, though, and it took centuries for a system of compulsory education to be established. Teachers, leaders, and parents had to campaign for years before reforms took place and the educational system we know today was established.

During the early days of education in the U.K., many students were schooled by local priests, who taught reading and writing classes in

5

Reading Skill:
Developing
Reading
Fluency

By focusing on general ideas while you are reading, and not on specific vocabulary, you will become a more fluent reader.

their churches. Few formal schools existed, and the ones that did were
costly and, therefore, reserved for children of the wealthy. In addition,
only boys were educated given the tradition that they would one day be
the family's sole breadwinner.

In 1187, England's first university, Oxford, was founded.[1] Over the next
400 years other colleges and universities were established including
Cambridge and Edinburgh. During the seventeenth century, numerous
private schools were founded and attended primarily by the sons of
aristocrats[2] who later continued their education at university. In the
centuries that followed, though, schooling for many still remained quite
haphazard; some pupils attended classes in churches, while others were
educated at Sunday school. Harsh punishments were quite common and
were given to disobedient or forgetful students. Education for the
majority of girls and young women consisted mainly of learning
domestic crafts; very few were exposed to the same academic content
that boys and young men were.

The lack of a formal system of teacher training became an increasing
issue, and in 1840, James Kay-Shuttleworth opened the first teacher-
training college. In 1846, he established the pupil-teacher apprentice[3]
system whereby pupils aged thirteen could study and serve for five
years with a teacher, then attend college for three years, in order to
become trained teachers themselves.

It wasn't until the late 1870s that laws were passed in the U.K.
requiring parents to ensure that their children received a basic
education in reading, writing, and math. In 1918, schooling became
compulsory up to the age of fourteen. The Education Act of 1944
reformed the schooling system further by providing equal educational
opportunities for boys and girls and changed teaching approaches to
incorporate students' individual ages and abilities.

In the late eighteenth and early nineteenth centuries, various pioneers in
educational reform were hard at work bringing about similar
improvements to the education system on the other side of the Atlantic.
Education in the U.S. at that time was much the same as it was in the
U.K., with badly equipped classrooms and untrained teachers. Horace
Mann was the first to establish teacher-training institutes; he also
campaigned for equal opportunities in education, and increased the
length of the school year from a few weeks to six months. John Dewey,
one of the most influential educational reformers of the twentieth
century, campaigned for alternative approaches to teaching in order to
accommodate a pupil's psychological and physical development, as well

as assist in academic progress. Dewey argued that classroom learning should center on the child, a belief that is now common practice in many classrooms around the world. Many of Dewey's theories continue to be discussed and debated by educators today.

50

Nowadays, a variety of schools exist in the U.S. and the U.K. Some offer basic academic education while others offer students the chance to specialize in their field of choice such as drama, science, music, or technology. Teachers must be fully trained and schools are required to follow government guidelines that specify which subjects should be taught in which grades. Today, educational content is regularly reviewed and adjusted in an effort to meet the changing needs of society and its learners.

55

60

---

¹ **founded** established or created an organization such as a school or business from the beginning
² **aristocrat** a member of the wealthy, usually noble, class; often related to royalty
³ **apprentice** person learning a skill or trade by working with a trained professional

---

Reading Comprehension: How Much Do You Remember?

A Decide if the following statements about the reading are true (*T*) or false (*F*). If you check (✔) false, correct the statement to make it true.

	T	F
1. Early educators taught students in churches.		
2. Years ago, only boys were educated because many were expected to become priests.		
3. Oxford and Cambridge Universities were established in the same year.		
4. James Kay-Shuttleworth is best known for being the first educator in the U.K. to graduate from university.		
5. In the early part of the twentieth century, a law was passed in England requiring children to attend school until the age of fourteen.		
6. Prior to Horace Mann's reforms, children in the U.S. attended school for only six months a year.		
7. John Dewey, one of the most important advocates for educational reform in the U.S., believed classroom learning should focus on the teacher.		

B Check your answers with a partner. Count how many you got correct—be honest! Then, fill in the Reading Comprehension Chart on page 202.

Vocabulary Comprehension: Odd Word Out

A For each group, circle the word that does not belong. The words in *italics* are vocabulary items from the reading.

1. *formal*   unauthorized   proper   official
2. optional   necessary   required   *compulsory*
3. improvement   *reform*   change   decline
4. chaotic   predictable   *haphazard*   disorganized
5. kind   *harsh*   gentle   understanding
6. conceal   advocate   promote   *campaign*
7. unimportant   leading   *influential*   powerful
8. *center on*   ignore   focus on   attend to
9. realize   *take for granted*   assume   presume

B Complete the article below using the words in *italics* from A. Be sure to use the correct form of the word.

> Ask many Americans planning to travel to a non-English-speaking country which language they will communicate in while visiting and, unsurprisingly, many (1)_____ that they will be able to use English. Perhaps this response isn't unusual, given that English is a language used for international communication. What is surprising, though, is that over the last thirty years, the U.S. has fallen significantly behind the rest of the world in foreign language learning. Reports published in recent years have offered (2)_____ criticism of U.S. students' foreign language skills, and many critics are demanding (3)_____ in foreign-language instruction.
>
> Today, many educational experts and (4)_____ political leaders are (5)_____ for improvements in foreign language instruction in the U.S. A recent study, conducted by the Center for Applied Linguistics in Washington D.C., offers suggestions for ways that foreign-language instruction might be improved:
>
> 1. *Begin foreign language instruction earlier.* In the U.S., the majority of students in both public and private schools do not begin (6)_____ instruction in a language other than English until about the age of thirteen or fourteen. In countries such as Germany, Austria, Morocco, and Thailand, official instruction in a second language is (7)_____ beginning between the ages of six to nine. Related research conducted in the EU suggests that students who learn a second language early on are more aware of other cultures and, overall, are stronger in their own first languages.
>
> 2. *Improve teacher training, and the methods used to teach students a second language.* Too many foreign language classes in the U.S. still (8)_____ the teacher and text, rather than on the students—and getting them to speak in the second language. The report suggests that we must move away from (9)_____ teaching practices and standardize instruction by training teachers to use communicative teaching methods.

C Read the passage in B again. Can you think of other suggestions to add to the article?

Vocabulary Skill:

The Root Word *form/forma*

In this chapter, you read the adjective 'formal,' meaning 'proper' or 'official,' and the noun 'reform,' meaning 'a change.' Both words include the root word 'form,' meaning 'shape.' 'Form,' sometimes also written as 'forma,' is combined with prefixes and suffixes to form many words in English.

Ⓐ For each word, study the different parts. Then, write the part of speech and a simple definition. Use the information on prefixes and suffixes and your dictionary to help you. Share your ideas with a partner.

Word	Part of Speech	Definition
1. format	_____	_____
2. informative	_____	_____
3. transform	_____	_____
4. deformed	_____	_____
5. conform	_____	_____
6. formulate	_____	_____

Prefixes
con- with, together
de- not
in- in, within, into
trans- across, change

Suffixes
-al/-ive/-ed (with adjs) like or relating to
-ate (with verbs) to make or become
-tion (with nouns) the state of something

Ⓑ Complete each sentence using the words from the chart. Be sure to use the correct form of the word.

1. That was a really _____ presentation the teacher gave on the history of English. I learned a lot.

2. Joshua refuses to _____ to his family's expectation that he become a doctor. He's studying graphic design instead.

3. Dying her hair from black to blond _____ Frances's entire look.

4. Many romance novels follow a standard _____: a couple falls in love, breaks up, then gets back together.

5. Smoking or taking drugs during pregnancy can cause a child to be born _____.

6. Have you _____ a plan yet for the presentation? Who is going to speak first? Who will present the summary?

Ⓒ Combine the root *form* with the suffixes and prefixes in A to create three more words. Write a sentence using each word.

1. _____

2. _____

3. _____

What Do You Think?

Discuss the following questions with a partner.

1. *Up to what age is education compulsory in your country?*
2. *What kind of formal training must a person have in order to become a teacher in your country?*
3. *If you could make changes to the educational system in your country, what would you change, and why would you change it?*

Real Life Skill

Common Academic Abbreviations

There are many common abbreviations used to refer to qualifications, or academic degrees, one receives after a period of study. These abbreviations are written as well as said, and when spoken, each letter of the abbreviation is pronounced.

(A) Practice saying each abbreviation. Then, match an abbreviation with the correct phrase.

Degree	Definition
1. B.A.	a. Master of Science
2. B.S.	b. Master of Arts
3. A.A.	c. Bachelor of Science
4. M.A.	d. Doctor of Philosophy
5. M.S.	e. Master of Business Administration
6. M.Ed.	f. Bachelor of Arts
7. M.B.A.	g. Associate of Arts
8. Ph.D.	h. Master of Education

(B) Write the appropriate abbreviation next to each description. Check your answers with a partner.

A person who graduates from a...	has a(n)
1. university with a degree in biology	_____
2. two-year junior, or community, college	_____
3. university with a higher degree in history, one level above a bachelor's	_____
4. university with a degree in English	_____
5. university with a degree in business, one level above a bachelor's	_____
6. university with a degree in engineering, one level above a bachelor's	_____
7. university with a degree of the highest rank, above a master's	_____
8. university or college with a degree in education, one level above a bachelor's	_____

The Mystery of Memory

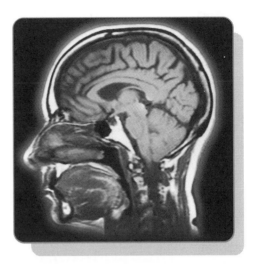

Getting Ready

Complete the survey below. Compare your answers with a partner.

1. Do you ever have trouble remembering people's names? ☐ Yes ☐ No
2. Do you ever forget important dates such as birthdays and anniversaries? ☐ Yes ☐ No
3. Do you remember what you did on your last birthday? ☐ Yes ☐ No
   How about on the day before that? ☐ Yes ☐ No
4. Do you often forget where you put things? ☐ Yes ☐ No
5. Do you ever forget to pay bills? ☐ Yes ☐ No

6. What were the last three movies you saw? Write them down.
   a. _____
   b. _____
   c. _____

7. Can you remember the names of the last three novels you read? Write them down.
   a. _____
   b. _____
   c. _____

8. Do you remember what you studied in your last English class? ☐ Yes ☐ No
   Write down two new words you learned.
   a. _____
   b. _____

Based on your answers to the questions above, do you think you have a good or bad memory? Explain your answer.

Before You Read:
Brain Power

Discuss the following questions with a partner.

1. How much do you know about the functions of the human brain?
2. Do you know anything about how memories are stored in the brain? What do you know about memory loss?
3. What are some of the things people do to improve memory?
4. The following words can all be found in the reading. What does each mean? How is each related to the topic of the reading?

retrieve   retention   sufficient
       recollect   stimuli

Reading Skill:
Skimming for the Main Idea

Skimming is one way to look for the main ideas in a reading. When we skim, we read over parts of the text very quickly. We don't need to read every word or look up words we don't understand; we just need to get a general idea of what something is about.

 Skim the passage quickly. Read only the *title*, the *first and last paragraphs*, and the *first sentence of each other paragraph*. Don't worry about words you don't know. Then, complete the sentence.

This reading is mainly about _____.

1. parts of the brain that store information
2. illnesses that result in severe memory loss
3. how humans process, store, and recall information

How Good Is Your Memory? _____

Some people have extraordinary memories. According to the Guinness World Records™, 2001, Gert Mittring of Germany can look at a list of twenty-seven numbers for just four seconds and remember all of them. Most people, though, have trouble at times remembering where they put 5 their door keys, or recalling the names of people they've recently met for the first time.

The process by which we store and retrieve information in our brains has been the focus of scientific research for many years. The brain is a highly complex organ that is not fully understood, and theories about how it 10 works remain a topic of debate. It is generally agreed, though, that one area of the brain known as the hippocampus—named after the Latin word for 'seahorse' because of its curved shape—is important in the process of recalling information. When we experience something, the information is sent via[1] our senses[2] to the hippocampus, where it is 15 processed.

Although the process of creating memories is only partially understood, it is thought to involve three main steps. Scientists believe that brain cells called neurons first transform the sensory stimuli we experience into images in our immediate memory. Then, these images are sent to the hippocampus and stored temporarily in short-term memory. In the hippocampus information is organized, and it is during this process that parts of the image of our experience fade away. Finally, certain information is then transferred to long-term memory in a section in the frontal lobe of the brain known as the cerebral cortex. Scientists think this process may happen while we are sleeping, but exactly *how* the information is transferred from one area of the brain to another is a mystery.

Although memory function is difficult to understand and analyze, memory loss is something that many people experience and worry about as they age. In the past, neuroscientists believed that age-related memory loss was associated with total numbers of brain cells. The theory was that the brain contained a finite number of neurons, and as we got older, we used up our stock of available cells. More recent research suggests that this may not be so and that neurogenesis, or the manufacture of new brain cells, may take place throughout a lifetime. Also, there is now evidence that damage to the hippocampus may play an important role in memory loss. Studies conducted on patients who have suffered damage to this area of the brain show that while they can still recall memories stored before the brain was damaged, they are unable to remember new facts. In addition, diseases associated with old age, such as Alzheimer's,[3] and other problems involving short and long-term memory loss, are now being traced[4] to possible damage to the hippocampus.

Research suggests that the power to retrieve information can be influenced by food and sleep. Vitamin E is, for example, able to break down chemicals, known as free radicals, that are thought to damage brain cells. Studies suggest that eating foods containing vitamin E, such as green vegetables, is one way of reducing age-related memory loss. Though there is no definitive proof, there are others who believe that herbs such as ginseng and ginkgo help to improve both concentration and memory retention. Research on short-term memory indicates that getting a good night's sleep can also help one to recollect things more clearly.

Although the exact process by which memories are coded and retrieved remains a mystery, there is no doubt that eating the right foods and getting sufficient amounts of sleep can help us make the best use of our brains' remarkable ability to store and recall information.

> 1 **via** by, by way of
> 2 **senses** the five senses: touch, sight, hearing, taste, and smell
> 3 **Alzheimer's** a disease that results in severe memory loss, behavioral problems, and, eventually, death
> 4 **traced** following a path or outline to find an answer

Ⓑ Now read the passage again, then answer the questions that follow.

Reading Comprehension: What Do You Remember?

Ⓐ How much do you remember about the reading? Complete the sentences with the correct information, then discuss your answers with a partner.

1. Some people such as Gert Mittring have _____.

2. This part of the brain plays an important role in information processing and memory: _____.

3. Information about an experience is first sent to the brain by way of our _____.

4. Brain cells, or _____, then transform the sensory information into images in our _____ memory. These images are then stored for a very brief period in _____ memory.

5. Information that we want to be able to recall in the future is moved to _____ memory, which exists in this part of the brain: _____.

6. In the past, doctors believed that memory loss was associated with _____. Today, however, research suggests _____ _____.

7. According to the reading, there is evidence to suggest that memory loss can be reduced by _____.

Ⓑ Using your answers to questions 3–5, explain the process that happens when a person touches a hot stove.

Vocabulary Comprehension: Odd Word Out

A For each group, circle the word that does not belong. The words in *italics* are vocabulary items from the reading.

1. *retrieve*	lose	regain	get back
2. recall	remember	forget	*recollect*
3. maintenance	*retention*	preservation	destruction
4. consequence	activator	*stimulus*	incentive
5. adequate	*sufficient*	enough	deficient
6. incredible	average	amazing	*extraordinary*
7. materialize	disappear	*fade away*	vanish
8. *finite*	limitless	unlimited	infinite
9. unsure	*definitive*	conclusive	certain

B Complete the sentences below using the vocabulary in *italics* from A. Be sure to use the correct form of the word.

1. The police have several theories but, at the moment, no _____ answer about the reason for the murder.

2. Do you think we have a _____ number of chairs for everyone attending today's meeting or will we need more?

3. I thought Dioni was at the party on Saturday night, but to be honest, I don't _____ seeing her there.

4. Do you think that the way a computer stores and _____ information is similar to how the brain works?

5. We have a _____ amount of time in which to complete this project—ten days, to be exact.

6. After a long economic downturn, tourism proved to be the _____ that improved the local economy.

7. The image appeared on the computer screen for a moment, then _____ and was lost for good.

8. During his illness, water _____ caused Renee's hands and ankles to become terribly swollen.

9. Carlos has an _____ ability to sleep only three hours a night and still be alert and attentive the next day.

Vocabulary Skill:

The Root Word *fic/fice*

In this chapter, you read the adjective 'sufficient' meaning 'enough.' This word is made by combining the root word 'fic,' meaning 'to do' or 'to make,' with the prefix 'suf-' and the suffix '-ent.' 'Fic,' sometimes also written as 'fice,' is combined with other root words, prefixes, and suffixes to form many words in English. Verbs that end in '-fy' are related to the root 'fic/fice.'

Ⓐ Match each root word or prefix with its meaning. Then, check your answers with a partner.

1. bene-		**a.**	to mark, to mean
2. de-		**b.**	great, large
3. magna		**c.**	under, beneath
4. pro-		**d.**	good, well
5. sign		**e.**	forward
6. spec		**f.**	not, away, down
7. sub-/suf-		**g.**	look

Ⓑ For each word, study the different parts. Then, write the part of speech and a simple definition. Use your dictionary to help you. Share your ideas with a partner.

Word	Part of Speech	Definition
1. sufficient	*adjective*	*enough, adequate*
2. beneficial		
3. deficit		
4. defy		
5. insignificant		
6. magnificent		
7. magnify		
8. proficient		
9. specify		
10. specification		

Ⓒ Complete the sentences using some of the words from the chart. Be sure to use the correct form of the word.

1. I saw a _____ exhibit at the Museum of Modern Art yesterday—some of the finest painting and sculpture I've ever seen.

2. Danny is _____ in two languages in addition to English.

3. Does the class syllabus _____ which unit we should read first?

4. In order to see a human cell with your eyes, you'll need to _____ it using this machine.

Think About It   Discuss the following questions with a partner.

1. *In English, a person with a good memory is said to have 'a memory like an elephant.' Do you have a saying like this in your language? Do you know anyone with an extraordinary memory?*

2. *Have you ever smelled or heard something that reminded you of something from your past? What do you think this tells us about how memory works?*

Discuss the following questions with a partner.

1. When you were a child, did you learn any rhymes or songs that helped you remember things like colors, numbers, or spelling rules?

2. What are some of the things you do to remember information that you will need to know for a test?

3. What are some of the things you do to learn and remember vocabulary in English?

4. The following words and phrases can all be found in the reading. What does each mean? How is each related to the topic of the reading?

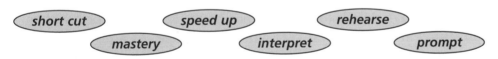

short cut   speed up   rehearse

mastery   interpret   prompt

Time yourself as you read through the passage. Try to read as fluently as you can. Record your time in the Reading Rate Chart on page 202.

Reading Skill:

Developing
Reading
Fluency

Words to Remember _____

People who have studied a foreign language know that it can be one of life's most rewarding experiences; they also know how much effort it takes. Faced with the prospect of endless hours of learning vocabulary, memorizing grammar rules, and practicing pronunciation, many people simply abandon hope of ever achieving a high level of fluency. Over the years, many students and teachers have developed useful shortcuts to make language-learning smoother, faster, and hopefully, more enjoyable.

> *By reading more fluently, reading will become easier. You will enjoy reading more if you feel it is easier.*

5

Remembering vocabulary necessary to express oneself in another language is the difficulty that many learners say causes the most anxiety. Expert opinions differ on the specific number of words a second-language learner needs to know to achieve mastery, but they generally agree that it is several thousand. Although it is possible to learn the meaning and usage of a large number of words, it can also be extremely time-consuming. One way that many teachers suggest accelerating the vocabulary-building process is by using mnemonics.[1]

Simply put, mnemonics is a method used to help one remember information that is otherwise difficult to recall. An example is the rhyme 'i before e, except after c, or when sounded like a, as in neighbor and weigh,' which many English learners use to remind themselves of a spelling rule. Mnemonics is based on the principle that by using as many functions of the brain as possible, information can be retrieved more easily.

The human brain interprets and processes tremendous amounts of information, some of which is used quickly and later forgotten. Some information, though, we want to store for later retrieval. Doing this often requires that we rehearse the information over time and in different ways. Much of the information we learn in school is often presented in only one way—as words on a page. As a result, many learners find that it is helpful to 'encode' the information they want to remember using rhymes, acronyms, or mental images.

Without even being aware of rhyming mnemonics, many English-speaking schoolchildren learn to count using a rhyme that begins 'One, two, buckle my shoe.' Many North American children memorize the names of the continent's Great Lakes by using the first letters of their names—Huron, Ontario, Michigan, Erie, and Superior—to spell out the acronym HOMES. Other learners use images such as graphs and charts to help them learn subjects such as mathematics or history.

Foreign languages are ideally suited to the use of mnemonics. One common mnemonic aid involves using images to link a word in your own language with a word in a foreign language. When learning French, for example, an English speaker might remember *tapis*, the

French word for 'carpet,' by imagining a rug with a tap or faucet as the central design. Another technique that learners use to recall foreign words is mind mapping. Using this method, a student might create a mental map of her hometown and link locations in the town to words she wants to remember. Nouns, for example, might be linked to buildings, adjectives with locations in a park, and verbs with activities at a sports center. The mental image of the town would act as a prompt and enable learners to recall the associated words.

Rhymes, acronyms, mental maps, and images are just some of the many types of mnemonic devices that can be used by language learners. Some students may still prefer to use flashcards or stick word labels on the furniture around their homes in order to learn vocabulary. The key, though, is to try a variety of methods and find a few that work best for you.

¹ **mnemonics** /nɪmɑnɪks/ named after Mnemosene, Greek goddess of memory

Reading Comprehension: How Much Do You Remember?

Ⓐ Decide if the following statements about the reading are true (*T*) or false (*F*). If you check (✔) false, correct the statement to make it true.

		T	F
1.	According to the reading, recalling vocabulary causes the most stress for language learners.		
2.	To be a successful speaker of another language, it is necessary to know millions of words.		
3.	A mnemonic aid is a mental strategy used by a learner to remember information that is hard to recall.		
4.	Mnemonics enable people to store information in one easy-to-reach part of the brain.		
5.	In order to store certain information in long-term memory, one often has to practice that information repeatedly.		
6.	HOMES is an example of a mind map.		
7.	For some learners, relating a word in their own language to a word in the new language helps them recall the new item.		

Ⓑ Check your answers with a partner. Count how many you got correct—be honest! Then, fill in the Reading Comprehension Chart on page 202.

Vocabulary Comprehension: Word Definitions

Ⓐ **Look at the list of words and phrases from the reading. Match each with a definition on the right.**

1. short cut   _____
2. mastery   _____
3. accelerating   _____
4. interpret   _____
5. rehearse   _____
6. prompt   _____
7. prospect   _____
8. abandon   _____
9. tremendous   _____

a. to desert or leave something behind

b. a stimulus; something that makes something else happen

c. a faster way of doing something

d. the possibility or likelihood of something happening

e. great skill; the ability to do something very well

f. a very large amount of something

g. to practice something in order to become familiar with or good at it

h. increasing the speed of something

i. to understand the meaning of something

Ⓑ **Complete the sentences below using the vocabulary from A. Be sure to use the correct form of the word.**

1. Before making our presentation tomorrow, I think we ought to _____ it once through.

2. If you take the _____ through the park, you'll arrive at my house faster than going through the city center.

3. There is _____ pressure on many high school students to study hard in order to enter a good university.

4. One way of _____ your reading speed is by not slowing down to look up every word you don't understand.

5. How did you _____ Consuelo's e-mail message? Did she seem angry to you?

6. Gabriel's _____ for getting into Harvard don't seem very good. He's only got a 3.0 GPA and isn't doing well in his classes this semester.

7. The car parked across the street has been there for over a week. My guess is that it was stolen and has been _____.

8. In order to receive an M.A. or M.S., one must first demonstrate _____ of his or her subject through oral and written examinations.

9. What _____ Leila to shout at Naoki in class today? I was really shocked.

Vocabulary Skill:
Vocabulary-recall Strategies

 A Review the different strategies you can use for associating and recalling vocabulary. Which do you commonly use?

> **Strategy**
>
> - **Word Association: linking one word to related words**
>   **e.g.:** *school-related words: teacher, student, classroom, books*
> - **Synonyms and Antonyms**
>   **e.g.:** *definitive—certain/unsure*
> - **Word Families**
>   **e.g.:** *attend, attention, attentive*
> - **Word Pairings**
>   **e.g.:** *hot coffee (not burning coffee)*
> - **Idioms**
>   **e.g.:** *a last resort*
> - **Root Words, Prefixes, and Suffixes**
>   **e.g.:** *the root fic/fice; the prefix re-*
> - **Mnemonic Aids**
>   **a.** *draw a picture that is related to the word or words*
>   **b.** *relate the sound or spelling of the new word to a sound or spelling in your own language*
>   **c.** *rhyme the new word with a similar word*
>   **d.** *relate the words to furniture in a room or places in a city*
>   **e.** *create a sentence or story using the words*
>   **f.** *combine all the words to make an acronym (e.g., HOMES)*

B Use one or more of the strategies above to help you recall the words below. Share your strategies with a partner.

memory	retention	short cut	deficit
memorize	short	recall	retrieve
accelerating	mnemonic	forget	device
memorization	elephant	beneficial	long-term

What Do You Think?

Discuss the following questions with a partner.

1. *As a second language learner, is remembering vocabulary the most challenging thing for you? How can you make it easier?*

2. *Do you think any of the techniques discussed in this chapter can help you to remember new vocabulary in English? Which ones will you use?*

Real Life Skill

Spell Check

In this unit, you've learned and reviewed some useful strategies for recalling vocabulary you learn in English. But what about spelling? In spite of the fact that one can use the 'spell check' feature on the computer, it is still helpful to be familiar with some of the basic rules for spelling in English. There are also several mnemonic aids one can use to recall the rules.

Ⓐ Review some common spelling rules in English. Say each of the words in the example column aloud.

RULE	EXAMPLE	TIP
IE or EI?	ceiling neighbor chief	I before E, except after C, or when sounded as A, as in neighbor and weigh.
Silent sounds	mnemonic psychology debt through tough	Circle or highlight the silent letter. Rhyme the word with another word—through-you; debt-jet to remember pronunciation.
Dropping the final E	care – caring careful	Words ending in silent E—drop the E if followed by a vowel (e.g., caring), but keep the E if followed by a consonant (careful).
Change Y to I	beauty – beautiful	Usually, words that end with Y after a consonant drop the Y and change it to I before adding a suffix.
Doubling letters	stop – stopped mail – mailed diner – dinner	Often (but not always!) long vowels take one consonant; short vowels, two.

Ⓑ For each pair, circle the word that is spelled correctly. Check your answers with a partner.

1. foreign   forin   **5.** timeing   timing

2. wieght   weight   **6.** accommodate   acommodate

3. though   thow   **7.** sunnyest   sunniest

4. recieve   receive   **8.** runing   running

Ⓒ Complete the spelling of the following words.

1. I was so embar_____ed when I tripped and fell. Everyone laughed at me.

2. Here's your r_____t for the coat you just bought. It was $150.

3. This person can predict the future: _____ic.

4. Can I use your k_____ to cut my meat?

5. Have you met my n_____e? She's my sister's daughter.

The Art World

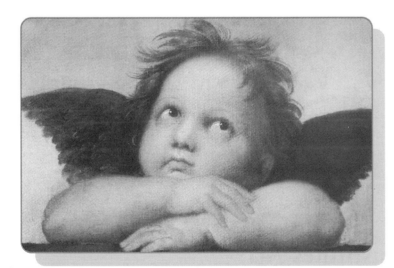

Getting Ready

Discuss the following questions with a partner.

1. *Look at the paintings above. Which of the artistic styles do you prefer? Why?*

2. *Do you consider all of these paintings to be works of art? Are there any that you do not consider to be art? Why?*

3. *How often do you visit art galleries and exhibitions? What kinds of exhibitions do you visit?*

4. *Do you know anything about the history of art? How many famous artists, living or dead, can you name?*

Before You Read:

Art History

(A) How much do you know about art and art history? Circle the correct answer to complete each statement.

1. Some of the world's earliest art was created in (small houses / caves / churches).

2. Michelangelo was one of the greatest artists of the (Classical / Baroque / Renaissance) era.

3. Art historians refer to today's artistic period as the (Premodern / Modern / Postmodern) era.

4. One of the artistic styles that many people today are discussing and arguing about is (Conceptualism / Pop Art / Surrealism).

5. The Turner Prize is an award given each year to (an American / a British / a Canadian) creator of an important piece of art.

6. In 2001, the winner of the Turner Prize was (Madonna / Andy Warhol / Martin Creed).

(B) The following words are all in the reading passage:

innovative   contemporary   denounce

perception   icon

What does each word mean? How does each word relate to the topic of art?

Reading Skill:

Scanning

When reading something to find certain information, we move our eyes very quickly across the text. When we 'scan' like this, we do not read every word, or stop when we see a word we do not know; instead, we read quickly, stopping only to find the information we need.

(A) Scan the reading to check your answers to the art history quiz above. How many did you get right?

(B) Read the passage again, then answer the questions that follow.

What Constitutes Art? _____

What is art? According to one definition, it is the creation of something that appeals to[1] our sense of beauty. This definition may include painting, drawing, sculpture, and architecture, or performing arts such as music and drama. Cultural and historical influences, as well as one's
5 own perception of what is aesthetically pleasing, play a role in what one believes to be art. To some people, art is the depiction[2] of an object—a painting or sculpture of a person, for example. For others, art may be a blank canvas, or a piece of chalk.

In order to talk about the different artistic styles that have existed over time, art historians have classified these styles into different periods and organized them in chronological order. The works of art produced within each period mirror[3] the culture and events of that time.

The earliest forms of art, from the Prehistoric era, include simple cave paintings and figures made from stone. These were followed by the sculptures and carvings of the Ancient Civilizations[4] era. Styles of the later Classical[5] era (800 B.C. to 200 A.D.), reflect the culture of the time—one that favored simplicity and balance. The period of the Middle Ages followed, and was succeeded by a revival of classical styles in the Renaissance era, beginning around 1400. Well-known artists of this time include Michelangelo and da Vinci. One hundred years of Baroque[6] style, and then fifty years of Rococo[7] followed the 200-year Renaissance. The start of the nineteenth century saw the rise of the Premodern era, followed by the Modern era, a period that lasted until 1945. This was followed by the Postmodern era that characterizes the present day.

In addition to differences in artistic styles *between* eras, there are also differences *within* each era. The Postmodern era, for example, has featured innovative artistic styles such as Pop Art (which includes work by Andy Warhol), Minimalism, and Conceptualism. Since the 1960s, Conceptualism has grown in popularity. This style focuses more on the idea or 'concept' of art using realistic objects, rather than on art that is created using traditional materials such as paint, canvas, stone, or clay. Whereas Warhol used a can of beans as the basis for a painting, for example, a conceptual artist might say that the can itself is a work of art.

Conceptualism has become an increasingly controversial art style, particularly as a result of numerous conceptual artists winning the Turner Prize. This £20,000 award is presented annually to a British artist under the age of fifty, in recognition of an outstanding work. Sponsored by the Tate Gallery of Britain, it is recognized as one of Europe's most prestigious[8] awards for visual arts. Its aim is to promote discussion about contemporary British art. In 2001, pop music icon Madonna presented the Turner Prize to conceptual artist Martin Creed.

Creed's winning work consisted of an empty room in an art gallery. Every five seconds the light in the room turned on, and then turned off again. Creed entitled this piece of art *Work # 227*. Other examples of Creed's work include *Work # 88*—a piece of paper crumpled into a ball. While some art critics have celebrated these works for their ability to make us question our surroundings and values, others denounce them as rubbish.

50 According to some, Creed's work explores the relationship between art, reality, and life. It is also thought to challenge the material value of traditional art. Creed believes that by using everyday objects, his work gains no monetary[9] value—unlike paintings that might eventually sell for millions.

55 While this explanation helps us understand the message Creed and other conceptual artists make with their work, the question remains—is it art?

---

[1] **appeals to** to be pleasing or attractive to something or someone
[2] **depiction** the description or representation of something
[3] **mirror** to reflect or represent
[4] **Ancient Civilizations** very old cultures, such as those of ancient Egypt and Mesopotamia
[5] **Classical** relating to the art, architecture, and literature of the ancient Greeks and Romans
[6] **Baroque** style of European art characterized by bold, elaborate curves
[7] **Rococo** style of decorative art that originated in France, characterized by elaborately detailed images of flowers, leaves, scrolls, and animals
[8] **prestigious** important, well-known, celebrated
[9] **monetary** related to money

Reading Comprehension:
What Do You Remember?

Ⓐ How much do you remember from the reading? Put the following artistic eras in chronological order from the oldest (1) to most recent (10).

The Middle Ages	_____	Baroque	_____
Postmodern	_____	Modern	_____
Ancient Civilizations	_____	Classical	_____
Renaissance	_____	Premodern	_____
Prehistoric	_____	Rococo	_____

Ⓑ Decide if the following statements about the reading are true (*T*) or false (*F*). If you check (✔) false, correct the statement to make it true.

	T	F
1. Pop Art, Minimalism, and Conceptualism are styles that developed in the Modern era.		
2. History, culture, and one's concept of beauty affect what a person believes to be art.		
3. Conceptualism is a style of art characterized by the use of traditional materials such as paint and clay.		
4. The goal of the Turner Prize is to encourage people to think and talk about modern British art.		
5. Almost everyone agrees that Martin Creed's *Work # 227* is excellent.		
6. Martin Creed thinks that his art will someday be worth millions.		

(A) Look at the list of words from the reading. Match each with a definition on the right.

1. constitute _____

2. classify _____

3. chronological _____

4. innovative _____

5. aesthetic(ally) _____

6. perception _____

7. contemporary _____

8. icon _____

9. denounce _____

a. inventive, new, original

b. one's belief or opinion about something

c. to divide and put into groups by type

d. modern, current

e. to criticize or condemn someone or something

f. to be, to compose or make something

g. relating to beauty

h. arranged in order of time, sequential

i. a famous person, usually one who symbolizes a way of life

(B) Complete the questions and statements below using the words from A. Then, answer the questions using your own information and discuss your answers with a partner.

1. Talk about a _____ artist (painter, musician, author) that you like. Explain why you like this person.

2. Why do you think that some people _____ artists like Martin Creed?

3. Other than Madonna, can you name another twentieth century _____?

4. Would you _____ the book *The Life and Times of George Washington* under history or science?

5. Put the following events from Pablo Picasso's life in _____ order: leaves school as a child because of an illness / paints the Guernica in 1937 / moves to Paris in 1904 / born in Malaga, Spain

6. What kind of art is _____ pleasing to you?

7. Imagine that you work for a language school in your city. Your company wants you to think of an _____ way that students can learn English. Discuss your idea.

8. Do you think that the media can influence people's _____ of world events? Give an example.

9. Do you think that air and water pollution _____ a threat to people?

Vocabulary Skill:
Homophones

In this unit, you read the noun 'canvas.' There is another word, 'canvass,' that is pronounced the same as 'canvas,' and spelled almost the same, but has a different meaning. Words like this are called 'homophones,' and there are many of these in English.

(A) Compare the words *canvas* and *canvass*. Use each in the sentences below. Be sure to use the correct form of the word.

> **canvas** /kænvəs/ *n* strong, thick type of cloth on which artists paint; also used to talk about a painting itself
>
> **canvass** /kænvəs/ *v* to gather people's opinions about something; to try get information by going from place to place

1. Police _____ the area where the car was stolen but were unable to find any information that could help them locate it.

2. How many of Martin's _____ are going to be on display at the Racine Gallery this weekend?

(B) Look at the pairs of words below. For each pair, write a sentence using the words correctly. Use the definitions to help you.

> 1. **role** /roʊl/ *n* the position or part one takes in a certain situation, e.g., in a play, at work, in a family
>
>   **roll** /roʊl/ *v* to move forward by repeatedly turning over, e.g., to roll a ball

_____

_____

> 2. **palette** /pælɪt/ *n* a piece of flat, round wood or plastic held in the hand, used to mix paints together *a painter's palette*
>
>   **palate** /pælɪt/ *n* the top of the inside of one's mouth

_____

_____

> 3. **idol** /aɪdl/ *n* a person that others love or respect; a hero or celebrity, e.g., a teen idol
>
>   **idle** /aɪdl/ *adj* inactive, lazy

_____

_____

Think About It **Discuss the following questions with a partner.**

1. *Do you think that Creed's conceptual work is art? Explain your answer.*
2. *Think about the aim of the Turner Prize. Do you think Creed deserved to win the prize? Explain your answer.*
3. *Why do you think Madonna was chosen to present the Turner Prize in 2001? Do you think she was an appropriate choice? Why or why not?*
4. *In your opinion, who is the most innovative artist of all time? Explain your answer.*

Chapter 2: Is Tattooing an Art Form?

Discuss the following questions with a partner.

1. Look at the picture above. Why do you think this person has tattoos?
2. Do you know how a tattoo is made?
3. What is a stereotype? In your country, what is the stereotypical image of people who wear tattoos? What is the stereotypical image of a tattoo artist, or *tattooist*?
4. The following words are all in the reading passage:

temporary   outcast   talisman
permanent   dropout

What does each word mean? How does each relate to the topic of tattoos?

Time yourself as you read through the passage. Try to read as fluently as you can. Record your time in the Reading Rate Chart on page 202.

> *By focusing on general ideas while you are reading, and not on specific vocabulary, you will become a more fluent reader.*

Is Tattooing an Art Form? _____

The practice of marking the human body with images and designs has existed in some cultures for thousands of years. Some markings are temporary, such as painting henna[1] on the hands and feet of brides in India, while others are permanent. The practice of leaving a permanent mark on the skin using needles and dye, or pigment, is known as tattooing.

The word *tattoo* originates from Polynesia where, on islands like Tahiti and Samoa, the tribal tattoo traditionally played a significant role in the organization and interaction[2] of the people. Ancient Maori[3] people

5

10 painted their faces with charcoal[4] before battles. Eventually, the markings were made permanent by tattooing so that they did not have to be reapplied before each battle. Warriors without these facial markings were referred to as 'plain face' and were considered social outcasts.

15 The Haida people, who inhabit the Queen Charlotte Islands near Canada, today still tattoo their hands and forearms with pictures of animals that signify their family name. In some jungle tribes of Borneo, a tattoo is viewed as a talisman and is worn to protect a person from harm and disease. Other indigenous cultures display bodily markings as
20 a kind of trophy[5] to signify success in hunting.

Today, tattooing is a common practice in many parts of the world. For some people, a tattoo is simply a form of body decoration; for others, it provides a symbol of cultural or group identity. Millions of people, including 30 million in the U.S. alone, have some form of tattoo on
25 their body. However, tattooing may also have a negative image; in Japan, for example, a common perception of people with tattoos is that they are associated with the Japanese mafia, or *yakuza*.

Many tattooists in Japan emulate classical Japanese artistic styles in their work. Throughout the world, in fact, tattooists are often referred
30 to as tattoo *artists*, and many studio employers insist that these artists have some kind of background or training in art before hiring them. Some tattoo artists will have taken university courses in art or related subjects before seeking employment. An artistic background and attention to detail are important for two reasons: first, as with
35 traditional tattooing in indigenous cultures, modern tattoos—for example, a person's astrological symbol or an image of a family member or close friend—may have special meaning to the wearer. The tattoo artist must be able to meet the exact requirements of his or her customers in terms of artistic style and aesthetic quality. Second,
40 because tattooing is a time consuming and often painful procedure, with results that are permanent, it must be done well artistically and very carefully.

The stereotypical image of the tattoo parlor as a dingy[6] backstreet shop is, in most cases, far from reality. A modern tattoo studio today is more
45 likely to look like a dentist's office, with waiting room walls adorned[7] with artwork. As needles are used in the tattooing process, cleanliness and hygiene are of the utmost importance. The National Tattoo Association in the U.S. has over a thousand members, and promotes the image of tattooing as a profession with high quality standards. The

stereotypical image of tattooists as rebel dropouts is gradually
changing. Instead, most tattooists today are regarded as professionals,
trained in the art and practice of tattooing. It is common for a tattoo
artist, in fact, to work as an apprentice for a few years with a
professional tattooist before working independently.

Millions of people around the world, many of them famous celebrities,
wear their tattoos with pride. For these people, a beautifully created
tattoo can be just as much an artistic endeavor as a work of art by a
Renaissance painter.

50

55

---

¹ **henna** reddish dye, obtained from the leaves of the henna tree of Asia and northern Africa
² **interaction** contact, communication, or relations between two or more people
³ **Maori** an indigenous, native people of New Zealand
⁴ **charcoal** a black, chalky substance, often used as fuel; sometimes used to draw with
⁵ **trophy** object or symbol of achievement or victory
⁶ **dingy** dark and dirty
⁷ **adorned** decorated

Reading Comprehension: How Much Do You Remember?

Ⓐ Choose the best answer for each question or statement below.

1. According to the reading, tattooing leaves _____ marks on the skin.
   a. lasting   **b.** short-term   **c.** henna

2. The word *tattoo* comes from _____.
   a. India   **b.** Polynesia   **c.** Canada

3. Which is NOT a reason listed in the reading that native people wear tattoos?
   a. for protection   **b.** for beauty   **c.** as a trophy

4. According to the reading, it is important for a tattoo artist to have _____.
   a. a tattoo and an art degree
   b. studied art and be attentive to detail
   c. a university degree and be an artist

5. According to the reading, which is often true about tattoos?
   a. It doesn't take long to have one done.
   b. People often get a tattoo that has personal meaning.
   c. Having a tattoo done isn't painful.

6. Today, many tattoo studios are _____ clean and hygienic.
   a. not at all   **b.** somewhat   **c.** very

7. According to the reading, many people _____.
   a. still hide the fact that they have a tattoo
   b. are starting to think of tattooing as an art form
   c. don't believe tattooing is a profession

Vocabulary Comprehension:
Words in Context

Ⓑ Check your answers with a partner. Count how many you got correct—be honest! Then, fill in the Reading Comprehension Chart on page 202.

Ⓐ The words in *italics* are vocabulary items from the reading. Read each question or statement and choose the correct answer. Compare your answers with a partner.

1. A *temporary* job will probably last _____.

    a. a few months   **b.** until you retire

2. Which of the following could cause *permanent* damage to a person's health?

    a. a cold   **b.** a heart attack

3. The Ohlone people lived in many parts of Northern California for thousands of years before the Spanish arrived in the mid 1700s. Who were the *indigenous* people?

    a. the Ohlone   **b.** the Spanish

4. A _____ person would probably carry a *talisman*.

    a. logical   **b.** superstitious

5. A _____ would probably be considered a social *outcast*.

    a. psychologist   **b.** *dropout*

6. If a young artist *emulates* a well-known artist's style, he _____ it.

    a. imitates   **b.** rejects

7. Which might be a *stereotypical* image of people from the United States?

    a. They are all rich   **b.** They come from many different places

8. _____ might be a challenging *endeavor*.

    a. Opening your own business   **b.** Going on holiday

Ⓑ Now think of other examples using the vocabulary from A. Discuss your ideas with a partner.

1. Why might a person take a *temporary* job?

2. Name something else that could cause *permanent* damage to a person's health.

3. What do you know about *indigenous* people in other parts of the world? How about in your own country?

4. Other than a tattoo, what might be an example of a *talisman*?

5. Why might a *dropout* be considered a social *outcast*?

6. Why might a young artist *emulate* another artist's style?

7. What is a *stereotypical* image others have about people from your country?

8. What else might be a challenging *endeavor*?

Vocabulary Skill: Nouns and Adjectives with *out*

A Match a verb on the left with a definition on the right. Then complete the sentences below. Be sure to use the correct verb tense.

1. speak out _____

2. hand out _____

3. burst out _____

4. stand out _____

5. come out _____

6. take out _____

a. to be obvious or noticeable to others in some way

b. to be a certain way in the end

c. to remove something from a place

d. to talk openly and honestly about something, usually in protest

e. to give or distribute something to others

f. to do something suddenly, usually with great emotion

In this chapter, you read the words 'outcast' and 'dropout.' These nouns are formed from the verbs 'cast out,' meaning 'to eject' or 'throw out,' and 'drop out,' meaning 'to leave or remove oneself from a situation, school or society.' Sometimes, verbs that are followed by the word 'out' can be used to form nouns and adjectives in English.

1. If you're going outside, could you _____ the trash?

2. When the teacher suddenly started singing loudly, the entire class _____ laughing.

3. Connie tried to paint a picture of Luke, but it didn't _____ very well.

4. Before I _____ the tests, I'd like to remind everyone that there is no talking during the exam.

5. The painting's bright colors really _____ against the dark background.

6. Students are going to _____ against the university's plans to cut many of the art and music courses.

B What do you think the following words mean? Use them to complete the sentences.

> handout   outspoken   takeout
>
> outburst   outstanding   outcome

1. Martina is one of the most _____ women I know. If she doesn't agree with something, she'll tell you.

2. I'm too tired to cook tonight. Can we order _____ from the restaurant instead?

3. Before she began her presentation, Hiroko gave everyone a _____ that summarized its main points.

4. I was shocked when Alex told Tina to shut up in front of the class. I thought his _____ was totally inappropriate.

5. Jin-hee really is a(n) _____ student. She's had excellent grades for three years in a row.

6. What was the _____ of your discussion with the professor? Will he let you turn in your paper late?

C Now indicate if the words in B are nouns (*n*) or adjectives (*a*) by writing *n* or *a* above each word. Discuss your answers with a partner.

What Do You Think?

Discuss the following questions with a partner.

1. *Do you think that tattooing is an art form? Why or why not?*
2. *Do you know anyone with a tattoo? Why did this person get a tattoo?*
3. *Imagine you are going to get a tattoo. What kind of tattoo will you get?*
4. *According to the reading, the stereotypical image of tattooing is changing, and today, many see it as an art form. Can you think of another stereotype that is changing today in your country?*

Real Life Skill

Art Appreciation

In this unit, you learned about different periods of art history. The chart facing includes some of the styles and artists that were popular within each era; they are referred to quite often in magazines, newspapers, literature, and other media. How familiar are you with these styles and artists?

(A) Complete the chart below with the missing information. Share your ideas with a partner. Can you think of any other artists to add to the chart?

Van Gogh	Renoir	Martin Creed	Holland
Salvador Dali	Pablo Picasso	Italy	Austria
Rembrandt	Andy Warhol	Mexico	The U.S.

Period / Style	Artist	Country
Renaissance / Baroque		
Renaissance	da Vinci	Italy
Baroque	Michelangelo	
	_____	Holland
Premodern to Modern		
Impressionism	Monet	France
	Cezanne	France
	_____	France
		_____
Expressionism	Gustav Klimt	
Cubism	_____	Spain
Surrealism	Man Ray	
	_____	Spain
	Frieda Kahlo	_____
Modern to Postmodern		
Pop Art	_____	The U.S.
Minimalism	Frank Stella	The U.S.
Conceptualism	_____	The U.K.

(B) Look again at the pictures in Getting Ready on page 157. Write three words that come to mind when you look at each. Compare your ideas with a partner, and explain your choice of words.

Modern Shakespeare

Getting Ready

Discuss the following questions with a partner.

1. *The man in the picture is a very famous English playwright. Can you name him?*
2. *How many other famous English-language writers, dead or living, can you name?*
3. *What kinds of literature do you like to read? Do you have a favorite play or novel?*
4. *Do you enjoy watching films that are based on books you have read or plays you have seen? Why?*

Before You Read:
Shakespearean Knowledge

Discuss the following questions with a partner.

1. Look at the title of the reading. How much do you know about this man's life?
2. Can you name any of Shakespeare's plays? Have you read any of them?
3. Why do you think people still read Shakespeare's work today?
4. The following words and phrases can all be found in the reading. What does each word mean? How is each related to the topic of the reading?

literary   authentic   cover-up

genius   plausible

Reading Skill:
Logical and Chronological Sequencing

Dates as well as words like 'first,' 'then,' 'next,' 'when,' 'after,' 'later,' and 'today' are often used in a reading to show a sequence of events. Being aware of how a reading is organized can help you to understand it better, and enable you to find specific information in a passage more easily.

Ⓐ First, skim the reading to get an idea of what it is about. Then, scan the reading and put the events in the chart in the correct order. List the year next to each event.

The Life and Times of William Shakespeare	
Event	**Date**
1. The First Folio is published	
2. Shakespeare marries	
3. Christopher Marlowe dies	
4. William Shakespeare is born	
5. The Earl of Oxford, Edward de Vere, travels to Italy	
6. Shakespeare dies	
7. Playwright Christopher Marlowe is born	
8. Edward de Vere dies	

Ⓑ Use the dates in the chart to help you decide who probably wrote the Shakespearean plays—Marlowe, Shakespeare, or de Vere? Why couldn't the others have written them? Explain your answer to a partner.

Ⓒ Read the passage again, then answer the questions that follow.

Who Was Shakespeare?_____

William Shakespeare is widely regarded as the greatest English language playwright. He was a literary genius whose works are still read and performed all over the world. Shakespeare, the man, is something of an enigma, though, as very little is known about him. We do know that a
5 William Shakespeare was baptized[1] on April 26, 1564, the third of eight children of John and Mary Shakespeare. He lived in the town of Stratford-upon-Avon in England and when he was eighteen, he married

a twenty-six-year-old woman named Anne Hathaway. They had three children, including one set of twins. For much of his life, he was employed as an actor in London, and he died in 1616, at the age of fifty-two.

Beyond those basic facts, little else is known about the life of Shakespeare. Even his birthday, April 23, is speculative and is based on the assumption that baptisms at that time took place three days after a baby's birth. In total, 154 sonnets[2] and 37 plays, which are grouped into comedies, tragedies, and histories, are attributed to William Shakespeare. However, not one original manuscript has survived; the plays and poems we know today come from a collection known as the First Folio, published in 1623 after Shakespeare's death. The only portrait of him accepted as authentic appears on the title page of the First Folio.

This lack of historical data has caused some literary experts to question whether William Shakespeare really wrote the works attributed to him. Skeptics cite a number of arguments to support their belief that Shakespeare, the playwright, was really someone else. First, fourteen plays have scenes that take place in Italy and demonstrate a detailed knowledge of Italian society and politics. However, there is no record of Shakespeare's ever traveling to Italy. Skeptics also argue that the level of vocabulary and language used in Shakespeare's works reflects the writings of a highly educated person with a good understanding of law, politics, and history. Yet there is no record of Shakespeare's ever attending a university.

If William Shakespeare did not write the great plays and sonnets, then who did? The two most plausible candidates are Edward de Vere, the 17th Earl of Oxford, a contemporary poet and friend of Queen Elizabeth I, and Christopher Marlowe, also born in 1564, a Cambridge graduate, playwright, and—allegedly—Elizabethan[3] spy.

Advocates for de Vere argue that his aristocratic background and travels throughout Italy in 1575 make him a likely candidate. However, de Vere died in 1604, and many of the greatest Shakespearean plays, including *King Lear* and *The Tempest*, appeared after this date. Also, there is no convincing explanation as to why de Vere might prefer to write using William Shakespeare as his *nom de plume*.[4]

As with the de Vere theory, a major flaw to the Christopher Marlowe theory is the timing of his death. Many historians believe that Marlowe was killed in a fight in a London pub in 1593. However, conspiracy[5]-

minded Marlowe experts argue that this was a cover-up and that he was secretly sent to Europe to work as a spy for Elizabeth I. Skeptics suggest that Marlowe continued to write, but used William
50 Shakespeare's name to enable him to get his work published in England.

Today, the majority of Shakespearean scholars believe that, in spite of his humble beginnings, the man from Stratford-upon-Avon was the true author of the literary greats.[6] They argue that Shakespeare's lack of
55 formal university education does not mean he could not have produced works of such genius. Until enough evidence is collected to firmly support any argument, debate surrounding who the Bard[7] of Stratford really was continues.

---

[1] **baptize** to perform the ceremony of baptism in which water is poured over a person to purify and welcome him into the Christian Church
[2] **sonnet** a type of poem with fourteen lines and a specific pattern and rhythm
[3] **Elizabethan** of, or relating to, the period in England during which Queen Elizabeth I reigned
[4] **nom de plume** French for 'pen name'—a fictitious name used in place of an author's real name
[5] **conspiracy** a plan to do something in secret
[6] **literary greats** works of literature of outstanding importance or significance
[7] **bard** an old-fashioned way of referring to a poet or storyteller

---

Reading Comprehension: What Do You Remember?

Decide if the following statements about the reading are true (*T*) or false (*F*). If you check (✔) false, correct the statement to make it true.

	T	F
1. Historians are certain that Shakespeare was born on April 23.		
2. One of the original manuscripts that Shakespeare wrote still exists today.		
3. The First Folio can also be described as Shakespeare's collected works.		
4. Some experts doubt William Shakespeare was the true author of the plays as he spent most of his time in Italy.		
5. Edward de Vere may have written *King Lear* and *The Tempest* before his death.		
6. William Shakespeare used a *nom de plume*.		
7. Some believe Marlowe did not die and went to live in Europe.		

Vocabulary Comprehension: Words in Context

Ⓐ The words in *italics* are vocabulary items from the reading. Read each question or statement and choose the correct answer. Compare your answers with a partner.

1. Your teacher hands you back a paper that has several *flaws* in it. In other words, there are some _____.
   a. suggestions   **b.** mistakes

2. Which of the following statements is *plausible*? _____
   a. There may be life elsewhere in the universe.   **b.** The Earth may be flat.

3. Yoko owns an *authentic* Van Gogh painting. In other words, it is _____.
   a. a copy   **b.** genuine

4. A *genius* is someone with _____ ability or talent in a field.
   a. average   **b.** extraordinary

5. Which is an example of a *cover-up*? Tom steals money from Mary _____.
   a. but pretends he doesn't know about it   **b.** but later tells her

6. A person with *humble beginnings* typically comes from a _____ family.
   a. somewhat poor   **b.** middle class

7. A *literary* critic typically gives his or her opinion about _____.
   a. books   **b.** film

8. The police *attributed* the fire to a cigarette. The cigarette was the _____ the fire.
   a. result of   **b.** reason for

9. Many critics *regard King Lear* as Shakespeare's greatest work. They _____ it is his greatest work.
   a. wonder if   **b.** believe

Ⓑ Complete the sentences using the words in *italics* from A. Be sure to use the correct form of the word. Then, take turns asking and answering the questions with a partner.

1. In your country, who is _____ as one of the greatest artists of all time?

2. Talk about someone you know who comes from _____, but has improved his or her position in life.

3. How might you prove that a painting or book is _____?

4. What are some of the great _____ works that you have read?

5. Many people think Albert Einstein was a _____. Do you think he was?

6. Can you think of any _____ reasons why very little is known about Shakespeare, in spite of the fact that he was a great playwright?

7. You notice that a jacket you like very much has a couple of _____ on the inside lining. There is only one jacket left for sale. Will you buy it?

8. Your uncle, a great but unknown writer, dies unexpectedly. You are also a writer, but not a very good one. After your uncle's death, some of his greatest stories are _____ to you. Would you mount a _____ campaign or admit that the stories are not yours?

Vocabulary Skill:

Word Combinations

In English, there are word pairs or groups of words that naturally go together. In this chapter, for example, you learned the verb 'regard.' This verb can stand alone, but in many sentences it is also often used together with the prepositions 'as' or 'with.' Becoming familiar with common word combinations can help you to better use and recall vocabulary you've learned.

Ⓐ Look at the examples below.

1. **Verb + Preposition**
   Some verbs are only used with certain prepositions.

   • Shakespeare is *regarded* **as** one of the great playwrights of all time.
   • Jane's parents *regarded* her announcement of marriage **with** surprise.

2. **Adjective + Noun**
   As you learned in earlier units, certain noun and adjective combinations work together to talk about one thing.

   • Let's get some *fresh* **air**.   • He is my *close / good / best* **friend**.

3. **Verb + Noun**
   Some nouns go with certain verbs to talk about one idea.

   • Who is going to *make* **dinner**?   • When will you *go* **shopping**?

Ⓑ Look at the words in the box below. What part of speech is each one? Match them with the nouns and prepositions to form some common word combinations. Some words will have more than one match. Use your dictionary to help you. Compare your ideas with a partner.

make	do	go	hard	short
think	move	hope	know	work

1. _____ a decision   4. _____ about   7. _____ of
2. _____ with   5. _____ time   8. _____ to
3. _____ for   6. _____ as   9. _____ work

Ⓒ Complete the paragraph below with the correct noun, verb, adjective, or preposition. Be sure to use the correct form of the word. Check your answers with a partner.

Very little is known (1)_____ Shakespeare's life between the years 1585 until 1592. After the birth of his twins, Shakespeare (2)_____ a big decision—to move (3)_____ London where he hoped (4)_____ support his family. Some people believe that for a (5)_____ time, Shakespeare worked (6)_____ a private teacher in Lancashire because he had a (7)_____ time finding other work. Others believe that in 1587, a famous theater group visited Stratford, and Shakespeare began working (8)_____ them. Shakespeare's quick wit and hard (9)_____ pleased the group. Thus began his life in the theater.

Think About It   **Discuss the following questions with a partner.**

1. *Do you believe that someone else may have written the works attributed to William Shakespeare? Why or why not?*

2. *Write a letter to the editor of a newspaper defending Shakespeare against the critics who think he is not the true author of the great works attributed to him. Share your letter with a partner.*

Before You Read:
Modern
Shakespeare

Discuss the following questions with a partner.

1. Which words would you use to describe Shakespeare's plays?
2. Have you ever seen any of Shakespeare's plays on stage, TV, or film? Did you enjoy the performance?
3. Do you know which of Shakespeare's plays have been adapted, or changed, for a modern audience?
4. The following words and phrases can all be found in the reading. What does each word mean? How is each related to topic of the reading?

- screenplay
- predominant
- archaic
- adapt
- backdrop

Time yourself as you read through the passage. Try to read as fluently as you can. Record your time in the Reading Rate Chart on page 202.

Reading Skill:
Developing
Reading
Fluency

> Reading fluently means getting the main idea of the material you are reading without slowing down to look up words in a dictionary.

Shakespeare in the Movies _____

Ask people what they think of Shakespeare's work and their answers will most likely contain an array[1] of adjectives: creative, exciting, confusing, inspiring, difficult. Millions know Shakespeare as the icon of Western literature, but more recently, he has also gained recognition as one of the biggest names in Hollywood. Though there are actors who have movie star appeal and a small group of directors who create the blockbusters,[2] when it comes to providing a great screenplay for a movie, Shakespeare stands alone.

5

Throughout the history of movie making, Shakespeare's plays have been adapted for film more than the works of any other author. Since the 1899 filming of a London stage production of *King John*, there have been nearly 200 movie versions made of *Hamlet*, *Macbeth*, and *King Lear* alone. In addition, many films, such as Japanese director Akira Kurosawa's *Ran*, are loose[3] adaptations of Shakespeare's work, while others, like *Star Trek VI: The Undiscovered Country*, include references to the plays. Though his work was originally written for the theater, it is clear that the Bard's influence extends far beyond the stage.

Over the years, many scholars have speculated that Shakespeare wanted his plays to entertain as well as educate, particularly with regard to social morals. In contrast, many filmmakers today have tended to put entertainment value first, particularly those in Hollywood. Although early big-screen versions of Shakespeare's plays were little more than filmed stage performances, it wasn't long before directors were exploiting cinema's unique strengths to produce adaptations that were both crowd-pleasers and works of art in their own right. Over the years, film producers have taken various approaches to Shakespeare, with some choosing the traditional approach in which characters dress in the clothes of the period in which the original play was set. This was the predominant style of the adaptations produced by the BBC[4] in the early 1980s; it was also the style used by Laurence Olivier in his Oscar-winning 1944 version of *Henry V* and in Franco Zeffirelli's 1968 film version of *Romeo and Juliet*.

Director Orson Welles was one of the first to take an alternative approach to Shakespeare with his 1936 version of *Macbeth*. Set in nineteenth-century Haiti,[5] Welles's *Macbeth* was one of the first Shakespearean film adaptations that used a contemporary setting and put a new spin on themes in the original work; a more recent example is a production of *Richard III* set in 1930s England. In the same spirit, director Baz Luhrmann used present-day California as the backdrop for his 1996 film version of *Romeo and Juliet*. Luhrmann exploited the powerful imagery of film to its fullest in order to make the complex, archaic language of the play easier for a modern audience to relate to.

With his 1998 film *Shakespeare in Love*, British filmmaker John Madden found yet another revolutionary way to interpret the great playwright and his works. Rather than simply adapting *Romeo and Juliet*, Madden based the story on an imaginary 'Will Shakespeare' character who, inspired by his love for an aristocrat's daughter, writes his first great tragedy. Cast with big name stars such as Gwyneth

Paltrow and Joseph Fiennes, *Shakespeare in Love* was a box-office hit and went on to win an Academy Award® for best picture.

50

Once feared by many high school students throughout the English-speaking world, Shakespeare's plays have taken on a new dimension[6] thanks to the creative forces of film. Popular movie stars have rejuvenated the stories of the great playwright, making them more fashionable. The most famous storyteller of all time looks set to remain an important force in filmmaking for many years to come.

55

---

[1] **array** a group or selection of something
[2] **blockbuster** a movie that is usually very popular, and remarkable in some way
[3] **loose** not exact or fixed
[4] **BBC** the British Broadcasting Corporation
[5] **Haiti** /heıti/ country in the Caribbean near Cuba
[6] **take on a new dimension** to seem new or different in some way

---

Reading Comprehension: What Do You Remember?

(A) How much do you remember? Decide if the following statements about the reading are true (*T*) or false (*F*). If you check (✔) false, correct the statement to make it true. Try not to look back at the reading for the answers.

	T	F
1. Christopher Marlowe has had more of his works made into films than Shakespeare.		
2. The earliest Shakespearean play made for film was *Hamlet*.		
3. Shakespeare primarily wanted his plays to provide a moral education for the general public.		
4. Many of the early film versions of Shakespeare's works were plays performed as they were originally written.		
5. Welles's film version of *Macbeth* and Luhrmann's *Romeo and Juliet* are examples of the traditional approach used by some directors.		
6. *Shakespeare in Love* was different from other movies in that it included the playwright as a fictional character.		
7. A recent production of *Richard III* was set in 1930s Haiti.		

(B) Check your answers with a partner. Count how many you got correct—be honest! Then, fill in the Reading Comprehension Chart on page 202.

Vocabulary Comprehension:
Word Definitions

A Match each of the words and phrases from the reading with a definition on the right.

1. screenplay _____

2. adapt _____

3. predominant _____

4. backdrop _____

5. archaic _____

6. morals _____

7. exploit _____

8. relate to _____

9. put a spin on _____

a. main or most obvious

b. ancient, dated, or very old-fashioned

c. to use something well for a specific purpose

d. a film's story and the script spoken by the actors in it

e. to change or adjust something so it is suitable for a given situation

f. to change information about something in order to make it seem new or different

g. a setting or environment

h. rules for good and bad behavior

i. to understand and feel connected to someone or something

B Complete the sentences below using the vocabulary from A. Be sure to use the correct form of the word.

1. In 1998, *Shakespeare in Love* won an Academy Award® for best _____ as well as best picture. Marc Norman and Tom Stoppard were the writers.

2. In 1995, *Sense and Sensibility* won the same award. Actor Emma Thompson _____ the script from Jane Austin's book of the same name.

3. The _____ _____ for most of the academy-award winning movie *Traffic* was Mexico.

4. When the Hollywood actor and his wife divorced, his manager _____ their separation saying that the couple were still very good friends.

5. Many educators today are trying to find ways to _____ the Internet for learning purposes.

6. Mark is a man without any _____. He would steal or lie if it could benefit him in some way.

7. Though arranged marriages were common in the U.S. at one time, today many Americans would consider this custom _____.

8. Cassandra loves her sister Eileen, but can't _____ her very well because Eileen is almost fifteen years older.

Vocabulary Skill:

Word Associations

(A) Think about the words *setting* and *backdrop*. How are these words similar? How about the words *film* and *blockbuster*? How are they related? How are they different?

(B) For each starter word shown below, use the vocabulary in the box to make associations. Some words can be used twice. Then, explain to a partner how the words in each group are related. Can you add other words or phrases to each association?

movie	stage	screenplay	actor	performance
playwright	director	backdrop	adapt	movie star
live	character	Hollywood	blockbuster	literary

film: _movie_ _____

theater: _____

(C) Use the starter words below to create your own word associations. Begin by saying the word to a partner. Your partner will reply with a synonym, or a related word. Continue until you have a six-word list. Share your associations with your classmates.

history: _____, _____, _____,

_____, _____, _____.

romance: _____, _____, _____,

_____, _____, _____.

career: _____, _____, _____,

_____, _____, _____.

(D) Now think of a new word or phrase and say it to your partner to begin an association. Who can continue for the longest?

> When you learn new vocabulary, it can be helpful to think about how words are associated, or related, with other words and phrases. When you form word associations, you connect words and phrases that are similar. Doing this can help you to more easily remember the meaning of new vocabulary.

What Do You Think?

Discuss the following questions with a partner.

1. *Have you ever seen any of the movies mentioned in the reading? What did you think of them?*

2. *Which would you prefer to see, one of Shakespeare's plays performed as it was originally written, or an adapted, modern version for the theater or film? Why?*

3. *If Shakespeare were alive today, how do you think he would feel about modern adaptations of his work? Explain your answer.*

4. *Can you think of any other books or plays that were written a long time ago, but have been adapted for a modern audience? How are the modern versions different?*

Real Life Skill

The Theater

In many parts of the world, theaters are places where people might see both films and live performances, such as plays or concerts. There are many common words and phrases used to talk about theater seating, tickets, and types of shows. Some of these, particularly in the U.S., are also used to talk about film showings.

Ⓐ Look at the words and phrases in the chart. How is each related to the theater? Tell your partner. Then, write the correct title for each word group in the chart.

Types of shows	Ticketing	During
Information about the show		

1.	2.	3.	4.
box-office balcony seats orchestra seats sold out VIP passes online booking concessions seat number	matinee evening show preview	intermission / interval Encore! audience curtain call	program venue event performance times duration auditorium

Ⓑ Complete each definition below with the appropriate word or phrase. Check your answers with a partner.

1. This is where you can buy your tickets. _____

2. An afternoon performance at the theater or movies; sometimes it costs less. _____

3. A break during a performance. _____

4. This gives you information about the story and actors. _____

5. You will see this sign if there are no more tickets available.

   _____

6. The best, and usually the closest, seats to the stage for a live performance. _____

7. You will hear people say this at the end of a great live performance.

   _____

8. These seats are one level above the floor, and are usually preferred for movie viewing, but not live performances. _____

9. This is a special performance or film screening shown early and open only to people with VIP passes. _____

Transport Innovations

1.

2.

Getting Ready

Discuss the following questions with a partner.

1. *What is an innovation? Can you name any recent innovations?*
2. *What are the innovations in the photos above called? How many other transport-related innovations can you name?*
3. *How do you usually travel short and long distances? Which method of travel do you prefer?*
4. *Can you name any famous inventors of transportation devices throughout history?*

Before You Read:

Modern
Transportation

Ⓐ Discuss the following questions with a partner.

1. Look again at picture 1 in Getting Ready. Why might someone use this form of transportation?

2. How do you think you use, or operate, this form of transportation?

3. What can we infer, or guess, from the statement below?

   In the early days of the automobile, only the very wealthy owned a car. Today, many people own cars; some own two or three.

Ⓑ Look at the title of the reading. How do you think the following words relate to the topic of the reading?

hype   ambitious   controversy

features   device   eccentric

Reading Skill:

Inferring

> Information in a reading passage is not always stated directly. Sometimes a reader has to infer, or make guesses, about events or a writer's opinion or meaning, from the information that is available in the reading.

Ⓐ Scan the reading quickly and choose the best answer to the questions below. You will have to infer or guess information from the reading. Explain your answers to a partner.

1. The media expected Dean Kamen's new invention to be something _____.
   a. smaller   **b.** more sophisticated   **c.** faster

2. Kamen is _____ about the future of the Segway.
   a. optimistic   **b.** reserved   **c.** pessimistic

3. Dean Kamen believes that the Segway might eventually _____.
   a. be faster than a horse and buggy   **b.** replace the car
   c. have four wheels

4. The author's view of inventors is that most are _____.
   a. heroic   **b.** ambitious   **c.** strange

Ⓑ Now read the passage again and answer the questions that follow.

The Segway—a New Look at Travel _____

When inventor Dean Kamen appeared on U.S. TV on December 3, 2001, to unveil his latest innovation, no one knew what to expect. Code-named 'IT' and kept top secret, Kamen's most recent invention had been a source of intense speculation and media hype for months leading up to its debut.[1]
5 Given the frenzy and excitement, a letdown was almost unavoidable. When 'IT' turned out to be little more than a motor scooter, many publicly expressed their disappointment. On closer examination, however, even Kamen's critics had to admit that the vehicle was an engineering feat.

The Segway Human Transporter looked more like a small lawnmower[2] than the next step in motorized transportation, but it did boast[3] some interesting features. The two-wheeled vehicle was designed for a single rider who would stand upright over its single axle and navigate using a set of handlebars resembling those on a bicycle. Riders controlled the Segway's speed and direction by shifting their weight, and thanks to gyroscopes[4] that kept the vehicle upright, there was no danger of falling down or being knocked over. Electrically powered, the Segway could travel over 15 miles on a single charge and reach speeds up to 12 mph.[5]

Although the Segway may not be a threat to its four-wheeled cousin in terms of comfort or speed, it was meant by its inventor to "be to the car what the car was to the horse and buggy." Ambitious plans for any inventor, but maybe not so unrealistic for a man with Kamen's vision and determination.

A college dropout and self-taught engineer, Kamen already held over 100 patents for his inventions when he developed the one he hoped would revolutionize short-distance travel. While still in college, Kamen started developing the medical devices that made his name,[6] eventually turning the modest R&D[7] firm he founded into a multi-million-dollar technology leader.

After creating innovations like the world's first portable insulin pump[8] for diabetics, Kamen shifted focus to the challenges faced by wheelchair users. In his view, the problem wasn't ineffective wheelchairs, but rather that the world was designed for able-bodied people. The inventor's high-tech solution to this was a robotic wheelchair known as IBOT that could go up and down curbs, traverse sand and gravel, and even climb stairs. This robot ended up paving the way for the Segway.

While creating IBOT, Kamen realized that the same technology could just as easily benefit people with full mobility. From there, it was a matter of developing a computer "that acts like your brain," a gyroscope "that acts like your inner ear," a motor "that acts like your muscles," and wheels "that act like your feet." The end product was a machine that answered the prayers of anyone who has ever suffered sore feet, bemoaned[9] the time it takes to walk downtown, or simply been too lazy to walk around the block to the corner store. Not everyone welcomed the Segway's arrival, though. Some complained it was too expensive, while others said it would further undermine the average American's fitness. A Japanese inventor even accused Kamen of stealing the idea for the Segway from him.

Despite the controversy, the U.S. postal service began using Kamen's invention a month after its unveiling, and a factory was built with plans to manufacture 40,000 Segways a month. The jury is still out on[10] whether the Segway will be remembered as the greatest invention since the light bulb, or 50 just another forgettable electronic device made by yet another eccentric inventor. For the forward-thinking individual, however, trips to the local supermarket will never be the same again.

---

1 **debut** first public showing or appearance
2 **lawnmower** a machine used to cut grass
3 **boast** to have something that is special
4 **gyroscope** a wheel located within a frame, used to keep something stable and balanced
5 **mph** miles per hour
6 **make one's name** to do something that makes one famous or well-known
7 **R&D** Research and Development, pronounced R-N-D
8 **pump** a tool used to move air or liquid from one place to another
9 **bemoan** to complain
10 **the jury is still out on (something)** not everyone has stated an opinion (about something) yet; a decision has not been reached

---

Reading Comprehension:
What Do You Remember?

Ⓐ How much do you remember from the reading? Choose the best answer for each question or statement below.

1. Before the Segway made its first public appearance in December 2001, it was known as _____.
   a. R&D
   b. IT
   c. IBOT

2. Which statement best describes the critics' reaction to the Segway?
   a. disappointing, but still an important achievement
   b. an expensive and disappointing technological invention
   c. a disappointing engineering mistake

3. Which is NOT a feature of the Segway?
   a. One person at a time can ride on it.
   b. Riders increase the speed by moving the handlebars.
   c. It is powered by electricity and can go up to twelve miles per hour.

4. Before Kamen created the Segway, many of his inventions were made for _____.
   a. the U.S. Postal Service
   b. the medical field
   c. technology companies

5. Some people reacted negatively to the Segway because _____.
   a. of its high cost
   b. it is difficult to use
   c. it may contribute to the ill health of some Americans

6. According to the reading, a computer is to the brain what a gyroscope is to the _____.
   a. muscles
   b. feet
   c. inner ear

7. Shortly after the Segway was unveiled, there were _____.

    a. no plans to do anything more with it

    b. plans to manufacture thousands of Segways every month

    c. hopes for a larger model of the Segway

Vocabulary Comprehension: Word Definitions

A Look at the list of words from the reading. Match each word with a definition on the right.

1. unveil	_____	**a.** to move across or through an area
2. hype	_____	**b.** debate or disagreement about something
3. feature	_____	**c.** to damage or weaken something over time
4. ambitious	_____	**d.** to reveal, show, or make known
5. device	_____	**e.** unusual, often in an interesting way
6. traverse	_____	**f.** public excitement about something
7. undermine	_____	**g.** having a strong desire to achieve success
8. controversy	_____	**h.** a tool, usually electronic, that is used for a particular purpose
9. eccentric	_____	**i.** a part of something; a characteristic or quality of something

B Complete the sentences below using the words from A. Be sure to use the correct form of the word.

1. I think it's pretty _____ to try and drive 1,500 miles in one day! I'm sure it'll take longer.

2. A fax machine is an electronic _____. Can you name another one?

3. There's been a lot of _____ about the company's plan to _____ their new product before the conference starts.

4. A lot of people thought that Orville and Wilbur Wright were a bit _____ when they said they were building a machine in which people would be able to fly.

5. This cell phone has a _____ that allows you to surf the Web, and send and receive e-mail.

6. There's been a lot of _____ recently about cloning human beings. Some people think it's okay; others think it's dangerous.

7. If you're planning to _____ the desert by car, you'll need one that moves quickly on sand and won't overheat.

8. Lying to your parents will _____ their trust in you.

Vocabulary Skill:

The Root Word *vers/vert*

In this chapter, you learned the words 'controversy' and 'traverse.' Both include the root word 'vers,' meaning 'to turn.' 'Vers,' can also be written as 'vert,' and combined with prefixes, suffixes and other root words to form many words in English.

(A) For each word, study the different parts. Then, write the part of speech and a simple definition. Use your dictionary and the information in the chart to help you. Share your ideas with a partner.

Vocabulary	Part of Speech	Definition
1. controversy	noun	debate or disagreement
2. introvert		
3. extroverted		
4. versus		
5. conversion		
6. anniversary		
7. vertigo		
8. revert		

(B) Complete each sentence using the words from A. Be sure to use the correct form of the word.

1. People who have problems with their inner ear will often experience _____.

2. April 6 is Kyle and Gina's first wedding _____.

3. Kenzo is a very outgoing and _____ person. He always seems to be surrounded by friends.

4. Did you see the soccer game on TV last night? It was Madrid _____ Rome, and the Spanish won!

5. If you don't want to _____ back to smoking, try chewing gum when you feel like you need a cigarette.

6. Jeffrey is an _____ who prefers his books to people.

7. After his _____ to Islam, Trevor stopped smoking and drinking alcohol.

Think About It   Discuss the following questions with a partner.

1. *You've seen a picture of the Segway and read about this invention. Would you buy one? Why?*

2. *Kamen believes the Segway will "be to the car what the car was to the horse and buggy." What does he mean by this? Do you agree or disagree with this prediction? Why?*

3. *Do you think that Kamen is an eccentric inventor or a great innovator? Why?*

4. *Imagine that it is the 1990s and Dean Kamen comes to you with his idea for the Segway. He asks you, a wealthy investor, to loan him money to develop and manufacture the device. Would you give him a loan? Explain your reasons.*

(A) Discuss the following questions with a partner.

1. What is the object in the picture above? What do people use it for? Do you know who invented it?

2. What does it mean if a person is 'ahead of his or her time'?

3. Can you name any individuals who were ahead of their time? What did they do?

(B) The following words can all be found in the reading. What does each word mean? How is each related to the topic of the reading?

| concept | | pioneer | | devise |
| astounding | | accomplished | | ignorance |

Reading Skill:
Developing
Reading
Fluency

Fluent reading means connecting thoughts and skills together. Focus on getting the gist. Use the skills you have learned, and don't stop reading if you don't understand.

Time yourself as you read through the passage. Try to read as fluently as you can. Record your time in the Reading Rate Chart on page 202.

Ahead of Their Time _____

On November 2, 1947, a crowd of onlookers at San Pedro harbor in Los Angeles witnessed aviation history. An enormous flying boat, nicknamed the *Spruce Goose*, sped across the bay and lifted 70 feet above the water. After just under a minute, it landed perfectly one mile down the bay. It was the first and last time the boat ever flew.

5

The original concept for construction of the *Spruce Goose* came from the need for more effective ways of transporting troops and materials from the U.S., needed to fight in World War II. Although the idea came from a man called Henry Kaiser, it was Howard Hughes, the legendary multi-millionaire, who actually developed the flying boat.

The most astounding thing about the *Spruce Goose*, in addition to its gigantic size, was its construction—it was made entirely of wood. Though it had promise, in the end, the project failed for three main reasons: the cost of building the enormous machine, the complexity of working with wood, and Hughes's perfectionist approach, which caused the entire project to finish behind schedule. The *Goose* was put into storage and remained hidden from view until 1976, when it was put on display for the public. In 1992, the plane was dismantled[1] and transported to Oregon,[2] where it remains today. Although mistakes were made in the construction of the *Spruce Goose*, many of its design features have been incorporated into modern cargo[3] planes. Like other pioneers in the field of transportation, Hughes was simply ahead of his time.

Centuries before Hughes was designing the *Spruce Goose*, another pioneer in transportation design was sketching plans for different kinds of flying machines. Leonardo da Vinci, perhaps the most famous artist of the Renaissance period, planned flying devices with flapping wings controlled and steered by human pilots. His research focused on the complex anatomy[4] of birds in flight, and he based his flying machines on this analogy. It took almost five hundred years for da Vinci's sketches to become real. In June 2000, a professional parachutist named Adrian Nicholas jumped out of a hot-air balloon over the South African countryside using a parachute made of wood and canvas based on one of da Vinci's designs. Nicholas landed safely and da Vinci's dream became reality. Leonardo da Vinci designed many other devices that are now used daily, including the helicopter and the underwater oxygen tank[5] used by divers.

The phrase 'ahead of his time' can be used to describe another inventor, Buckminster Fuller, who, like Hughes and da Vinci, was accomplished in many fields, including engineering, mathematics, cosmology,[6] and poetry. One of Fuller's most famous designs was for the geodesic dome, which has been defined as the lightest, strongest, and most cost-effective[7] structure ever devised. Over 300,000 geodesic domes are being used today as shelters, or to house delicate radar equipment and weather stations. A geodesic dome made of aluminum was used to house the *Spruce Goose* at Long Beach Harbor.

Fuller was one of the earliest pioneers of renewable energy resources such as solar, wind, and wave power, and he incorporated these into his designs. At the time of his research, he estimated that the total energy needs of humans could be met using natural sources of energy and claimed that "there is no energy crisis, only a crisis of ignorance."

50

Pioneering inventors such as da Vinci, Hughes, and Fuller paved the way for many devices and apparatus used today. If many of their designs did not bring them commercial success in their lifetimes, it is simply because they were ahead of their time.

55

---

¹ **dismantle** to take something apart
² **Oregon** Pacific Northwest state located north of California, in the United States
³ **cargo** goods for sale carried from one place to another by ship, plane, train
⁴ **anatomy** structure of the body
⁵ **oxygen tank** container carrying air
⁶ **cosmology** the study of the origin of the universe
⁷ **cost-effective** the best price that one can pay for something

---

Reading Comprehension: How Much Do You Remember?

Ⓐ How much do you remember from the reading? Decide if the following statements about the reading are true (*T*) or false (*F*). If you check (✔) false, correct the statement to make it true. Try not to look back at the reading for the answers.

	T	F
1. The reading talks mainly about three great innovators in transportation.		
2. The *Spruce Goose* was one of the first airplanes ever to fly.		
3. One of the most interesting things about the *Spruce Goose* was that it was made of lightweight metal.		
4. Although the *Spruce Goose* wasn't a success originally, many of its design features are used in aircraft today.		
5. Howard Hughes developed an early flying machine based on the drawings he had made of birds in flight.		
6. The geodesic dome is considered one of the strongest but heaviest structures ever made.		
7. Buckminster Fuller believed that humans could use waves, wind, and sun to generate all of the energy they need.		

Ⓑ Check your answers with a partner. Count how many you got correct—be honest! Then, fill in the Reading Comprehension Chart on page 202.

Vocabulary Comprehension: Odd Word Out

Ⓐ For each group, circle the word that does not belong. The words in *italics* are vocabulary items from the reading.

1. *witness*	miss	see	observe
2. thought	idea	device	*concept*
3. unexpected	*astounding*	predictable	surprising
4. follower	innovator	*pioneer*	leader
5. difference	*analogy*	similarity	comparison
6. knowledgeable	skilled	uneducated	*accomplished*
7. invent	· create	*devise*	copy
8. *crisis*	celebration	emergency	extreme difficulty
9. awareness	*ignorance*	knowledge	intelligence

Ⓑ Complete the sentences using the words in *italics* from A. Be sure to use the correct form of the word.

1. With more people moving into the city, but fewer apartments available, San Francisco is now facing the most serious housing _____ in its history.

2. Did you know that Wei plays the violin? In fact, she's quite an _____ musician.

3. The police are asking anyone who _____ the store robbery to come forward with information.

4. Complete the following _____: north is to south as east is to _____.

5. I can't show you a model of my new invention because it's still in the _____ phase. I can draw you a picture, though.

6. One of the _____ in the field of online communication is Tim Berners-Lee, the man credited with inventing and developing the World Wide Web.

7. You'll find that prejudice is often caused by a combination of fear and _____.

8. There were a(n) _____ number of people at the concert. We originally expected there to be 100, but about 950 arrived!

9. Noah has _____ a road plan that will take us from New York to Miami in four hours, but I don't think it will work.

Ⓐ Look at these two idioms related to time. What is the difference? Complete the sentences with the correct idiom.

Ⓑ Using the sentences to help you, write a simple definition for *ahead of time*.

ahead of one's time: too modern or forward thinking for the time period one lives in

ahead of time: _____

1. I thought Marcus was coming at 8:00, but he arrived _____ at 7:30.

2. Amelia Earhart was one of the first female aviators. She was truly _____.

Ⓒ Now do the same for each of the idiom pairs below. Compare your answers with a partner.

1. *at a time*: in a certain specific number
   at one time: _____
   a. Okay everyone; please enter the theater two _____.
   b. Ms. Yang lived in Taiwan _____, but she doesn't anymore.

2. *in no time*: _____
   in time: after a certain amount of time has passed, usually a while
   a. We're almost at the beach; it's only about another mile. We'll be there _____.
   b. Don't worry! You'll learn to write well in Chinese _____, but it'll take a while.

3. *all the time*: happening continuously, regularly
   of all time: _____
   a. I think that Thomas Edison is one of the greatest inventors _____.
   b. My computer keeps crashing _____, and I can't make any progress with this report.

4. *for a time*: for a short period of time
   for the time being: _____
   a. You can sit at Hannah's desk _____, but when she comes back, you'll have to move.
   b. Junko and Koji dated _____, but I don't think they are still together.

Vocabulary Skill:
Idioms with *Time*, Part 2: Inferring Meaning from Context

In this chapter, you read the idiom 'ahead of one's time.' An idiom is a fixed group of words that has a special meaning. There are many idioms that are formed using the word 'time.' Sometimes it's possible to know what the idiom means by looking at the individual words, but it can also be helpful to look at the surrounding words in order to understand its meaning.

What Do You Think?

Discuss the following questions with a partner.

1. *Which of the pioneers talked about in this unit was the most interesting to you? Why?*

2. *Can you give an example of a pioneer who wasn't successful in his or her lifetime, but who has influenced our lives today?*

3. *Think about Buckminster Fuller's statement, "There is no energy crisis, only a crisis of ignorance." What does he mean by this? Do you agree with his opinion? Why? Give an example to explain your answer.*

4. *With a partner, think of a concept for a new invention. Draw a simple sketch of your idea, and write a short paragraph about what it does and how it can help people. Share the idea with your classmates. See how many people will offer to loan you money to create your invention.*

Real Life Skill

Rules of the Road: International Signs

In this unit, you learned about inferring, or understanding meaning that is not stated directly in words. Every day, we understand meaning from things like road signs that use only symbols and not words. Many signs are international, but some are specific to certain countries.

Ⓐ Look at the signs below that are commonly used in the U.S. What do you understand each one to mean? How many of these are common in your country? Tell your partner.

a. b. c. d.

e. f. g. h.

i. j. k. l.

Ⓑ Now match each of the signs above with the meanings below.

1. First aid / hospital ahead _____
2. Pedestrian crossing _____
3. Accommodations / lodging _____
4. No parking _____
5. One way only _____
6. Buckle up / wear a seatbelt _____

7. Food / restaurant _____
8. Traffic merging from the right _____
9. No entry _____
10. Disabled access / parking _____
11. No U-turns allowed _____
12. No left turn allowed _____

Ⓒ Think of some other common road signs that are used in your country. What do they mean?

Vocabulary Index

Skills Index

Reading Skills

Vocabulary Skills

Real Life Skills

Atlantic Ocean

Pacific Ocean

Calgary
Vancouver
Oregon
Ottawa
Toronto
Chicago
New York
Washington D.C.
San Francisco
Louisville
Los Angeles
Atlanta
Havana
Haiti
Mexico City
Kingston
San Juan
Caracas
Panamá
Bogotá
Lima
La Paz
Brasília
Easter Island
Rio de Janeiro
São Paulo
Asunción
Santiago
Montevideo
Buenos Aires

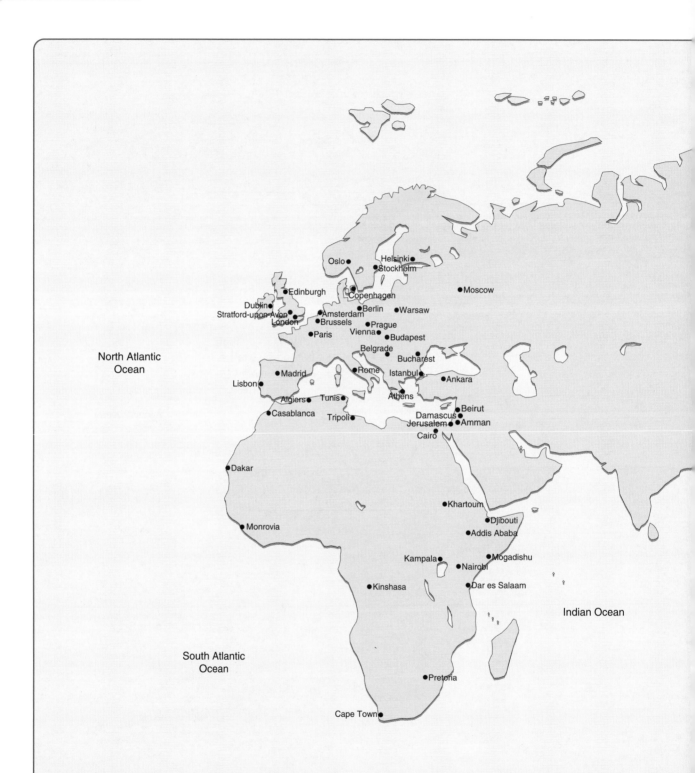

North Atlantic
Ocean

Oslo
Helsinki
Stockholm
Copenhagen
Moscow
Edinburgh
Dublin
Berlin
Warsaw
Stratford-upon-Avon
Amsterdam
London
Brussels
Prague
Paris
Vienna
Budapest
Belgrade
Bucharest
Madrid
Rome
Istanbul
Lisbon
Athens
Ankara
Algiers
Tunis
Beirut
Casablanca
Damascus
Amman
Tripoli
Jerusalem
Cairo

Dakar

Khartoum
Djibouti
Monrovia
Addis Ababa
Kampala
Mogadishu
Nairobi
Kinshasa
Dar es Salaam

South Atlantic
Ocean

Indian Ocean

Pretoria

Cape Town

Asia & Oceania

Ulan Bator

Beijing
Pyongyang
Seoul
Tokyo
Shanghai

Tehran
Kabul
Baghdad
Islamabad
Kuwait
New Delhi
Manama
Abu Dhabi
Riyadh
Dubai
Doha
Muscat
Calcutta
Hong Kong
Taipei
Pacific Ocean
Bombay
Hanoi
Yangon
Manila
Bangkok
Phnom Penh
Ho Chi Minh City
Colombo
Kuala Lumpur
Singapore
Indian Ocean
Jakarta
Port Moresby
Darwin
Cairns
Tonga
Perth
Sydney
Canberra
Adelaide
Auckland
Melbourne
Wellington
Christchurch

Reading Rate Chart

Time \ Unit	1	2	3	4	5	6	7	8	9	10	11	12	13	14	15	16	Rate (words per minute)
01:00																	600
01:15																	480
01:30																	400
01:45																	343
02:00																	300
02:15																	267
02:30																	240
02:45																	218
03:00																	200
03:15																	185
03:30																	171
03:45																	160
04:00																	150
04:15																	141
04:30																	133
04:45																	126
05:00																	120
05:15																	114
05:30																	109
05:45																	104
06:00																	100
06:15																	96
06:30																	92
06:45																	89
07:00																	86
07:15																	83
07:30																	80
07:45																	77
08:00																	75
08:15																	73
08:30																	71
08:45																	69
09:00																	67
09:15																	65
09:30																	63
09:45																	61
10:00																	60

Reading Comprehension Chart

Score \ Unit	1	2	3	4	5	6	7	8	9	10	11	12	13	14	15	16	%
7																	100
6																	86
5																	71
4																	57
3																	43
2																	29
1																	14
0																	0